2011

Happy Birthday Lon Yu

Grandma

D0575968

CHINESE EMPERORS

CHINESE EMPERORS

FROM THE XIA DYNASTY TO THE FALL OF THE QING DYNASTY

Ma Yan

FALL RIVER PRESS

This 2009 edition published by
Fall River Press, by arrangement with Compendium Publishing Ltd.

Fall River Press
122 Fifth Avenue
New York, NY 10011

ISBN-13: 978-1-4351-0408-2
ISBN-10: 1-4351-0408-0

Printed and bound in China

1 3 5 7 9 10 8 6 4 2

Project manager: Ray Bonds
Designer: Cara Rogers
Author and translator: Ma Yan
Historical fieldwork: Qu Yan
Photos by: Qu Yan, Robin Abecasis, Ma Yan and The Palace Museum,
Color Reproduction: Anorax Imaging Ltd

Page 1: Zhu Qiyu became Emperor Ming Jingtai while his brother Zhu Qizhen was being held prisoner by the Mongols.

Pages 2-3: The throne at the Hall of Supreme Harmony, the Forbidden City, Beijing.

Pages 4-5: A model of Kaifeng, thought to have been the world's largest city in the Song Dynasty.

Contents

Introduction

Five thousand years, a thousand leaders and emperors, and hundreds of dynasties indeed make for a lengthy story. I was searching for the highlights of individual periods and people when I started writing about the emperors. Instead, I was drawn into every event, every act of creativity, every form of brutality and savagery that resulted in China's progress over the centuries.

There are innumerable crowning moments in the long history of the nation, concerning the emperors as well as their people. Any judgment on individual emperors' successes or failures would not have been fair. No specific period or group of people is more important than another. It would not be pertinent to worship or admire merely Confucius and the Qing porcelain, without also considering the written and unwritten details from yesterday and before. They are as lustrous as the gold ornaments in palaces, and as paramount as each piece of sediment from the Yellow River at the heart of China.

This book could only ever be a broad brushstroke on the long scroll of China's history that continues to unfold. It begins with a brief description of each of the major dynasties, followed by concise pen-portraits of the most important emperors and leaders of the relevant periods.

Left: A dragon in the Forbidden City, the Chinese imperial palace in the center of Beijing. The dragon, an ancient mythical creature, symbolized power and authority.

The Major Dynasties

PREHISTORY–XIA DYNASTY
(C. 21ST CENTURY BC–17TH CENTURY BC)

Although Chinese history can be traced back to as early as the 21st Century BC, much of what we know of it is based on legend and mythology. The "Three Sovereigns and Five Emperors" led people who lived by the Yellow River to early civilization by teaching them fishing, farming, and husbandry as well as advocating partnership by marriage. Yan and Huang were the most respected two emperors and Chinese people often refer to themselves as their descendants. During this period of time, there were already legends and early signs of Chinese people counting days in a year and lunar cycle, practicing silk production, and even using needles for curing diseases.

SHANG DYNASTY
(C. 17TH CENTURY BC–11TH CENTURY BC)

The Shang was one of the more developed of the many tribes that lived downstream of the Yellow River. They were more advanced in husbandry compared to other tribes. The first kingdom was believed to have been established in Hao (near modern-day Shangqiu in Henan Province). The capital was later moved to Yin (today Anyang, Henan Province) during Pangeng's reign. Therefore it is also referred to as Yin Shang Dynasty.

From the bronze artifacts of the Shang period and the earliest form of Chinese characters inscribed on bones and turtle shells, we can conclude that the Shang already grasped many skills such as animal taming, fish farming, and land cultivation for survival. While the green bronze works mark the level of the Shang industrialization, stone sculptures found in Anyang reveal glimpses of the Shang lifestyle at the time: masters of slaves are shown wearing thin hats, pointed shoes, robes, and long skirts tied with wide belts. Music and dance were appreciated in court, but ruling depended on superstitious beliefs enforced with military power.

WESTERN ZHOU DYNASTY (1046 BC–771 BC)

The Zhou Clan lived west of China, close to today's Xi'an in Shanxi Province. Later they migrated towards the east and built their capital in Luoyang Henan Province. Around the 11th Century BC, they grew stronger and their political stability boosted the economy as well. The leaders established distinguished laws, thus further strengthening their ruling. In 841 BC, however, pressure from King Li triggered people to rebel, which brought an end to this empire based on family clans and instead ushered in the concept of a republic state.

Following King Xuan's prosperity, his son King You inherited the reign and became one of the most tyrannical emperors in Chinese history. His actions, coupled with natural disasters, meant that the empire couldn't sustain itself. In 771 BC, it ended by King Ping relocating the capital to Luoyi (modern-day Luoyang).

The political ideals, social rituality, and legality estab-

Left: Pottery from the Chinese Yangshao tribe (7000 BC–5000 BC)

lished during the Western Zhou Dynasty were much admired later by Confucius. His philosophy formed Chinese virtues and became fundamental to Chinese social standards. It has also deeply influenced many countries in East Asia.

EASTERN ZHOU DYNASTY (770 BC–256 BC)

Instead of a centralized dynasty, this era is better known as Spring and Autumn (Chun Qiu) (770 BC–403 BC) and Warrior (Zhan Guo) (403 BC–221 BC). The names Spring and Autumn came from a book edited by Confucius. According to the book, although the central Zhou reign existed with almost 140 sovereigns around China over three hundred years, the authority of the emperors was weakened by the growing independence of the regional monarchs. The starting year of King Ping and the 43rd year of King Jing are marked as the beginning and end of this era.

The following period, the Warring States, was much less peaceful. A set of written documents called *Archives of the Warring States* brought about its name. The central Zhou empire administration was shaken by more and more dukes in their regions declaring independence. Society at the same time was also reshaped due to a major industrial change: replacing tools made of heavy bronze with iron. Many schools of thought were circulated among monarchs and scholars. Some philosophies are still worshiped by Chinese and in other parts of the world today, such as Confucianism and Daoism.

Right: An imperial tomb found in Luoyang, where the remains of an unknown dignitary were found with a six-horse cart/carriage. Such burial arrangements were intended to show the person's superiority, a practice dating back to the Eastern Zhou (770 BC–256 BC).

QIN DYNASTY (221 BC–206 BC)

Among the seven Warring States, Qin was one of the strongest. Between 230 BC and 221 BC, Qin demolished the other six: Han, Zhao, Wei, Chu, Yan, and Qi. For the first time China appeared as a united country of many provincial groups. The central ruling also implemented various policies, such as aspects of currency, units of measure, and language to standardize the nation. Even the Great Walls were joined to protect China as one country. Laws were passed during the Qin, with amendments that lasted for almost 800 years until the Tang Dynasty.

However, the aggressive development and harsh policies aimed at strengthening central imperial power caused the society of mainly farmers to rebel. The first farmers' rebellion was widely echoed around the nation and eventually brought down the dynasty.

WESTERN HAN DYNASTY (202 BC–9 AD)

The Han Dynasty inherited many of the political ideals and strengthened the imperial system that was established by the Qin Dynasty. The leaders chose Daoism as their governing philosophy. Since China was united as one country, invasions from the barbarians in the west had always been a top priority. From the Han Dynasty, emperors relied on marriage as a diplomatic means to prevent war with the neighboring tribes. Stability boosted economy not only inside China but also encouraged trade to the surrounding countries. China has astronomic records dating as far back as the Han Dynasty and it is also believed that acupuncture and papermaking were already practiced.

Left: Terra-cotta warriors found underground near a tomb used during the Qin Dynasty (221 BC–206 BC).

Above: A mural found in the Han Dynasty tomb reveals how well-off people of the period traveled.

XIN DYNASTY (8–23 AD)

The Xin was a single-emperor dynasty, which became the transition period from Western Han to Eastern Han. It was set up for innovation. But due to unsuccessful economic reforms, the Emperor was overthrown and China fell back to the Han monarch.

EASTERN HAN DYNASTY (25–220)

The Eastern Han was established by the same monarch as the Western Han and therefore preserved many of the same policies. Reforms from the new administration revitalized the economy. Papermaking allowed writing to become more convenient than books written and threaded on bamboo, thus encouraging reading and writing. The Chinese language no longer looked like symbols but appeared as a formation of characters. Economy, culture, and scientific development far exceeded what the Western

Han Dynasty had achieved. Clay and pottery craftsmanship freed people from heavy metals, especially the bronze works. As well as natural herbs being used to cure illnesses, the *Book of Later Han* also described physician Hua Tuo as having applied a mixture of herbs and wine functioning as anesthesia during surgery.

THE THREE KINGDOMS: WEI, SHU, WU (184–280)

After a few farmers' rebellions, Wei, Shu, and Wu formed a triangle of equilibrium in North, West, and East China. Each held strong authority in his regions.

Among the Cao family, Caocao was the chancellor of the Han emperor. He declared himself King of Wei in 216. His son Cao Pi forced the Han emperor to give up his reign, calling an end to the Han Dynasty.

Liu Bei, King of Han, decided to continue the Han legacy and became the new Han emperor himself in 221. Sun Quan, originally a courtier of the king of Wei, aligned Han against Wei and declared their independence as the Kingdom of Wei in 229.

During this time the Chinese language advanced not only as communication but also as an art form. More poets appeared, including Caocao himself and his family members. Daoism was less popular and Buddhism was on the rise from the West.

WESTERN JIN (265–316) AND EASTERN JIN (317–420)

The Sima family started the Jin Dynasty and finished 100 years of the triangular dominance. In the meantime, nomadic tribes in the west from central Asia developed themselves and headed to the east, threatening China's western border again. An increasing number of tribal populations settled within China. The Western Jin was ended and the remains of the family inaugurated the Eastern Jin in South China. Within central China, nomadic settlers brought the western elements. The integration between east and west created a new and more tolerant culture.

FIVE HU'S AND SIXTEEN KINGDOMS (304–439)

The Chinese often abbreviate this period of time as the Sixteen Kingdoms. These kingdoms can be grouped into two eras: first half, Shu, Han, Zhao, Post Zhao, Yan, Qin, Liang; second half, Post Qin, Post Yan, Southern Yan, Northern Yan, Post Liang, Southern Liang, Western Liang, Northern Liang, Western Qin and Xia. In addition, there were kingdoms such as Dai and Wei of the Xianbei clan, as well as the Chinese Western Yan which were not accounted for in earlier history studies.

Regions in the west, especially the ones less at war, attracted more residents and caught up with development in agriculture and economy. Communication and cultural exchange escalated. This was when the Silk Road came into existence. Rulers, in order to stabilize their authority, encouraged cultural education and promoted religions.

SOUTHERN DYNASTIES: SONG, QI LIANG, CHEN (420–589)

Before China was reunited as one country, from the scattered sixteen-plus kingdoms, a few key kingdoms occupied the south and north regions. In the south, four dynasties were established by the Chinese. They occupied the areas from south of the Yellow River to the banks of the Yangtze River. The industrial development boomed in a few key cities in south China. They maintained and reinforced Chinese culture. The four main cities were Jian Kang (today, Nan Jing, Jiangsu Province), Jiang Ling (Hubei Province), Yangzhou (Jiangsu Province), and Chengdu (Sichuan Province).

Previous pages: Generally, each shift of reign in China's regional and unified history was initiated by conflict. This painting depicts Zhang Fei, who fought under Liu Bei in a battle against Zhang He under Cao Cao in 215 during the prelude to the Three Kingdoms Period. Liu Bei emerged victorious against Cao Cao's forces.

NORTHERN DYNASTIES: BEI WEI, BEI QI, BEI ZHOU, AND MORE (386–581)

The Northern Dynasties were Chinese kingdoms led by the nomadic Xianbei leaders. Therefore, Chinese culture was well preserved, adding influences from the Xianbei nomadic culture. In contrast with the southern detailed and elaborate literature, the Northern Dynasties left us with realistic, simple, and widely favored poems by the working class, such as *The Poem of Mulan*. The growth of these dynasties was fundamental to the booming Sui and Tang Dynasties that followed.

NORTHERN ZHOU DYNASTIES (507–556)

The Northern Zhou Dynasty was a sovereign of twenty-five years, managed through only five emperors. When they defeated the Northern Qi, North China was close to unification. Their success built a basis of the Sui Dynasty, which united China again as one country. Like many other co-existing states, the Northern Zhou Dynasty was also ruled by the Xianbei people, who adopted the Chinese system over a short period. But Emperor Yuwen Tai was more willing to preserve the Xianbei culture than Tuoba Hong; for example, he reversed some of the Xianbei names. Ruling, however, was still managed according to Chinese bureaucracy. He also believed in Confucian principles and instituted Confucius schools in the North.

SUI DYNASTY (581– 618)

The Bei Zhou emperor transitioned his kingdom to a new dynasty called Sui. The empire increased in size and the leaders carried out reforms to reduce bureaucracy. Additionally, a national examination system was instituted to recruit more talented people into joining the court.

To strengthen their military force, soldiers were enlisted as professionals and offered good benefits for themselves and their family members. Laws were clearly and more simply written in twelve sections and 500 terms, abandoning a great portion of harsh punishments. The Great Canal was excavated to connect north and south. By the end of the Sui Dynasty, the nation had reached a recorded population of 8.91 million.

TANG DYNASTY (618–907)

China progressed into an unprecedented prosperous time during the Tang Dynasty, making it the most developed country in the world at the time. Not only were its culture, politics, economy, and diplomacy advancing, but also these influences traveled to neighboring countries like Japan and Korea. With many countries willing to be courtiers of the Tang sovereignty, its borders reached as far as Korea in the east, the Aral Sea of mid Asia in the west, and Vietnam in the south. The combined territory was about eight million square miles, and the population exceeded 48 million.

Cultural exchange via the Silk Road and offshore sea trading became common practice. Not only did Chinese products such as tea, silk, and medicines, along with agricultural and technical skills including astronomy, papermaking, and printing, become introduced to foreign countries but also China gained knowledge in spices, gems, and Islam as a new religion. The Tang emperors were tolerant about religious beliefs; Buddhism and Islam became the two major religions in the country.

FIVE DYNASTIES AND TEN STATES (907–979)

During the transition from the Tang to Song Dynasties, there were five short dynasties followed by ten regional governments. The most significant achievements of this period were various books including Buddhist scripts, popular poems, and classical paintings.

NORTHERN SONG DYNASTY (960–1127)

The Northern Song policy was very much biased towards literary development. The leaders wished to avoid war. At the beginning of the 10th Century, the empire nations remained at peace. But their military weakness attributed to the downfall of the empire. According to Chinese historians, the Northern Song Dynasty was the greatest in Chinese history, ahead of the Tang Dynasty. Productivity is believed to have been twice as much as it was in the most prosperous times in the later Qing Dynasty.

Printing with movable typesets was invented, contributing to a flourishing publishing industry. For the first time, gunpowder was produced for military use. Policies, biased towards intellectuals, elevated freedom of speech and creativity. A new writing style between poems and songs, called "Ci," became a linguistic and performing art. The volume of trade reached a new level, bringing early capitalism to Chinese society.

SOUTHERN SONG DYNASTY (1127–1279)

The Southern Song Dynasty continued its military policy to avoid war, gaining success in trading and literature. After the Western Xia Dynasty in the west blocked the inland Silk Road, overseas trading was mainly via the sea routes, therefore improving nautical techniques as well as economic trading. An adapted version of Confucianism and Daoism appeared.

WESTERN XIA DYNASTY (1058–1227)

Western Xia was originally established by Dang Xiang people, who were a nomadic tribe from far west China (today, around Ning Xia Province). One of their main industries was pottery, a skill they learned from the Chinese. Although they had their independent language called Fan and their own educational system, their leaders largely copied the Song Dynasty to administer their own society.

YUAN DYNASTY (1271–1368)

The Xia were not the only people who copied the Chinese. The Mongolians blueprinted the Southern Song Dynasty for their Yuan before demolishing it with military force, thus ruling China for themselves. They employed Chinese Confucians as advisers in court. However, to prevent the Chinese from advancing in the Yuan society, Chinese were listed only as the third grade in the hierarchy. They were the first country in the world to use paper currency. During Kublai Khan's reign, the Italian traveler Marco Polo visited and resided in China before publishing *The Travels of Marco Polo* in Europe. This book and the Khan's massive conquering of Asia and Eastern Europe made the Yuan Dynasty famous around the world. The openness of the leaders and their policies promoted an epic assimilation of Western cultures and religions to the Chinese. China, as the world's largest nation, was robust but found it hard to sustain herself.

MING DYNASTY (1368–1644)

The Ming leaders perfected Chinese imperial dictatorship by defining the borders of the country and adding agencies to spy on their own people. Silver from the Americas became one of the standards for monetary exchange. Overseas trading with the Western countries also imported some modern military weapons to China.

During this period the imperial Chinese ideals were firmly strengthened. Women on the one hand were expected to have bound feet and yet were allowed to be educated. Printing and publishing flourished and there were as many as 1,239 state libraries. The first private library also appeared during the Ming Dynasty. Many long fictional works as well as scientific and technical publications marked the advancement of society.

SHUN DYNASTY (1644–1646)

The rebellion leader of the farmers, Li Zicheng, brought down the Ming Dynasty and inaugurated himself as the emperor of the Shun Dynasty. Once capitalized in Xi'an, western China, he moved the capital back to Beijing after a short time, to finish the Ming Dynasty by force. Two years later, the Manchurians invaded Beijing, ending this short-lived dynasty. Li Zicheng was exiled.

QING DYNASTY (1644–1912)

Manchurians originally were one of the strongest Mongolian clans in northern China. They had their own language and nomadic culture. From 1616, their first Khan Nurhachi had started to invade the northern border of the Ming Dynasty. In 1644, they easily marched into Beijing, then changed the name of the state to Qing.

Qing emperors admired Chinese culture and respected the Chinese in many aspects. For example, all emperors obeyed the Aisin Gioro (Aixinjueluo) family rule to study the Chinese language as well as their own Mongolian language. However, to maintain Manchurian superiority, the Chinese were ordered to follow the attire of the Manchurians.

The Qing Dynasty produced a few of the most hard-working and responsible leaders in Chinese history, such as Emperors Kangxi and Qianlong. Society within these reigns reached most prosperous levels. Their prosperity, however, was not comparable to the speed of the industrial development happening in Europe at the same time. In 1840, the European guns and cannons awakened this

sleeping dragon, forcing the Qing government unfairly to open trade. Many attempts towards the end of the dynasty to introduce reforms to catch up with the West failed, and the empire could not be rescued. In February 1912,

Emperor Aisin-Gioro Puyi signed his resignation statement marking the end of the Qing Dynasty, as well as Chinese imperialism. China then started to transform herself into a republic state.

Above: An exquisite clay model of imperial court performers dating from the Tang Dynasty (618–907).

THE EMPERORS

The equivalent word for "emperor" in Chinese is "Huang Di." As in English, it is a superior title rather than a name. However, in Chinese it is often mixed with emperors' names. For example, Emperor Han Wu in Chinese is called Han Wu Di, the "Di" referring to his title as an emperor. Emperor Tang Ming, in Chinese, is called Tang Ming Huang. Huang and Di originally carried different meanings in ancient Chinese: Huang meant the light and the heaven; Di meant the master of the living.

Qin, the first emperor, combined them together to declare he was the first to unite China. Huangdi became one word, and gradually the meanings of each individual character faded. Unless used to refer to specific names, Huang and Di are always combined as one phrase meaning emperor.

This process went through many phases, and it was a long process. After the remarkable Qin Dynasty unification there were no long-reigning emperors but kings, lords, masters, and saints. They were rulers or leaders, although

Left: The Great Wall of China was built, rebuilt, and maintained from the 6th Century BC to the 16th Century AD primarily to protect the northern borders of the Chinese Empire. Stretching for about 4,000 miles, there were, in fact, several walls, joined at various places and times.

here, in this brief introduction to the Chinese state leaders, we call them all emperors.

How many were there in China's history? Even that it is hard to define. Today, the term "Chinese" is a broad sense of people from China or whose ancestors were from China. Within today's China, there are Han Chinese, Mongolian Chinese, or even tribal leaders. This came about because before today's China there were many periods when people from many directions ruled under one Chinese dynasty. The Yuan Dynasty, for example, is one that is well known for having conquered massive territories.

The cultural integration and assimilation are what made Chinese culture prolonged and fascinating. It is a culture of a greater China, a country of many cultures. It is within this greater China that there were so many emperors or state leaders. We have summarized only a few in this book.

So what do we call these emperors? Ninety-nine percent of people would admit to having been confused by a Chinese name. Chinese names are art. A family name carries its family culture and tradition, while a given name carries hope, wishes, and expectations. Often they are also symbols of a generation. For example, a three-character name

often starts with a family name, followed by a generation character, and finally the given name. The generation character means everybody of the same generation within an extensive family could have the same character. Last but not least, many educated people in history have added an attached name (or sometimes two or three attached names) to their existing names. They could be much better known by their attached names than their original.

To confuse things further, emperors could be referred to by their names, era, reign, memorial name, or posthumous names. Some were better known for their era name and some could be better recognized by their memorial names, which were given by the next generation of emperor to name the tombs where the emperors were buried. On the other hand, Dowager Ci'xi was only referred to by her name as used in court. This is how she is best known, and she was certainly the exception in history. After all, not only did she rule China, she also lived across periods of four emperors, appointing two of them.

We have not referred to all versions of emperors' names because our intention was to look into who they were, rather than their delicate names of many forms. In Dowager

Ci'xi's case, the posthumous name is Empress Xiao-Qin Ci-Xi Duan-You Kang-Yi Zhao-Yu Zhuang-Cheng Shou-Gong Qin-Xian Chong-Xi Pei-

Tian Xing-Sheng Xian. There are a total twenty-three characters, all graceful.

Above: The throne at the Hall of Supreme Harmony, the Forbidden City, Beijing.

PREHISTORY–XIA DYNASTY
(21st Century BC–17th Century BC)

Fu Xi
Other name: Tai Wu

Fu Xi is a legendary figure who was depicted as having a human form on his top half, and a snake's body on the bottom half. He may have been married to his sister, who gave birth to their children. They were from the first tribes in China, located around the Yellow River.

He was the first "human being" mentioned in Chinese written archives since he was very well regarded among his tribe members, teaching them fishing, cooking, and hunting. He may have been the first "person" who counted numbers by using the binary system. The legend of him finding markings on dragon and turtle shells led the Chinese to think that they could be the very first appearance of Chinese calligraphy in primitive form. Chinese regard him as the Father of Civilization.

According to the earliest written Chinese legend, the world was a state of mist; Yin and Yang were divided. Fu Xi was the master of Yang and Nv Wa ruled Yin. Since he was thought to have been created from a snake, a simplified form of dragon, Fu Xi was also considered as the first descendant of Dragon.

Left: The legendary Fu Xi.

Right: The legendary Fu Xi is said to have been inspired by the swirls on the River Luo to create Bagua, also known as I Ching. These swirls are on a stone displayed in the Longma Temple, established in 348 to commemorate Fu Xi's creation.

Above: The Yellow River (Huang He), China's second longest river (after the Yangtze) is approximately 3,400 miles long. It is often referred to as the "cradle of Chinese civilization" and also "China's Sorrow" because of frequent devastating flooding.

Right: Calligraphic symbols on a replica of the Luo Stone.

Nv Wa

(pronounced Nuuu Wah)
Other name: Feng Lixi

Apart from the legend that she was the sister of Fu Xi, another popular folk story about Nv Wa describes her using the clay from the banks of the Yellow River to sculpt human figures. Later these figures became "human beings." Today, in some regions in China, she is worshipped as the goddess of marriage. Even though she figures in many popular stories about how she had bred and nurtured early "human beings," her name has never appeared in any written archives of Chinese history except for folk stories.

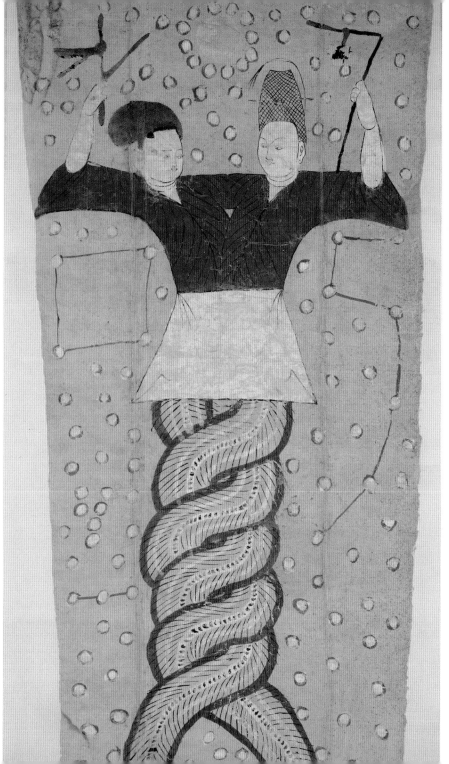

Right: Nv Wa, according to legend the first heroine in history, entwined with Fu Xi to create man and woman.
(The Palace Museum)

Yan Di

There are many memorials to Yan Di around China. It is said that he was one of the tribal leaders living over four thousand years ago, and was named Yan Di (the Emperor of Fire) because he took power by using fire. Records of the *Grand Historian*, the first Chinese historical archive, mentioned that Yan Di was the last leader of the Shennong tribe, possibly a female-dominant society for whom lamb was their main source of meat. It is possible that many of the early social behaviors already existed, such as cultivating five kinds of grains, using herbs, market trading, listening to musical instruments, using arrows crafted as weapons to maintain power, using simple stencils made from clay, and counting days, nights, months, and seasons.

Below: Yan Di, the last leader of the Shennong tribe, shown in a sculpture in a shrine in Luo Yang, Henan Province.

Huang Di

Huang Di was said to be the "Emperor of Clay." People say that he taught his people to turn raw food into cooked food by utilizing fire, and to weave raw materials into clothing. In his tribe there were also observations of the sun and moon and it is possible that the earliest lunar calendar was developed among his tribes.

According to legend, his wife Luo Zuo mastered the process of silk production and organized his people to produce silk in large quantities in order to clothe the rest of the tribe. Huang Di had twenty-five sons and each one of them was entitled to a share of some of the lands and the family wealth.

A popular saying related to the Chinese medical system is that Huang Di could have used needles to cure diseases, which is the earliest form of acupuncture that the Chinese can trace back to.

Below: Huang Di, also known as the Yellow Emperor, is said to be the ancestor of all Han Chinese. This sculpture of him is in a shrine in Luo Yang, Henan Province.

Yao

Yao is said to be the descendant of Huang Di. Today, people also call him Tang Yao, since he was from the Tang tribe. When he was leader of his region, there could have been a serious flood and Yao appointed Yu to be in charge of the project of flood diversion along the Yellow River.

In Chinese historical archives it was clearly stated that up to Yao's time the tribal system, rather than imperial rule, was still the fundamental of society. But there were signs that Yao commenced some implementation of state policies, to appoint commanders for individual tasks, for example. It is believed that during Yao's time Chinese people followed the four-season cycle, the lunar cycle, and a solar cycle of 366 days for agricultural guidance.

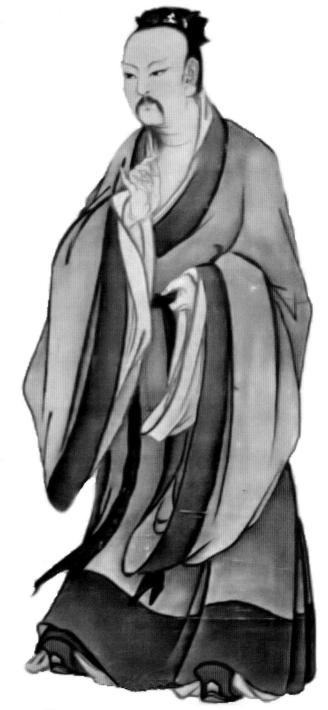

Right: Using artistic license, this is how Chinese people imagined what Yao looked like.

Yu

Yu is usually regarded as Great Yu (or Yu the Great) in the Chinese language respectful form, and was possibly the first emperor of the Xia Dynasty. He was said to have come from a well-off family background. Yet, when leading the project of the flood diversion, he was devoted, diligent, and creative.

He traveled far to carry out extensive research on the source of the Yellow River, then he led people to construct channels from the river to divert the flood. At the lower end of the river, he also taught people to take advantage of previous floods for agricultural needs and to create fields along the channels for irrigation.

He also instituted the Law of Yu, which could have been the commencement of a slavery system in China. Even though the stories describe these events from four thousand years ago, various recent historical researches have proved the legend to be close to what really happened.

Right: Yu, also known as Yu the Great, is regarded as a descendant of Huang Di, and is best remembered for his teachings on flood control techniques.

SHANG DYNASTY
(c. 17th Century BC–11th Century BC)

King Shang Zhou
(1075 BC–1046 BC)
Name: Xin Zishou

Emperor Shang Zhou was described as tall, smart, and having super-human strength as compared to ordinary people. Records of the *Grand Historian*, one of the earliest archives tracking Chinese history at the start of the century, stated that Emperor Shang Zhou enjoyed his wine, and partied throughout the night with men and women running around naked. It is also stated that he led his army towards the southeast to expand his territory to the Yangzi River.

Left: The Battle of Muye (1046 BC) southwest of Yin, central Henan, culminated in the end of the Shang Dynasty and the beginning of the Zhou Dynasty. The corrupt Shang Zhou armed over 100,000 slaves to guard his capital, but he had treated them badly and they defected to King Zhou Wu.

Left: A three-legged wine pitcher, made in brass during the Shang Zhou era; Shang was apparently fond of the contents.

Above: Shang Zhou suffered defeat by King Zhou Wu at the Battle of Muye, in which it is said all of Shang's forces were slaughtered.

But his cruelty brought the empire down. King Zhou Wu led 300 battle carts, 3,000 warriors, and 45,000 soldiers to attack Shang, whose army mainly consisted of prisoners and slaves. They met in Muye and fought one of the largest battles during that period, but King Zhou Wu triumphed by a wide margin since the soldiers who had been tortured by Shang Zhou were unwilling to fight for him.

WESTERN ZHOU DYNASTY
(1046 BC–771 BC)

King Zhou Wen

(1152 BC–1056 BC)
Name: Ji Chang

King Zhou Wen led the prosperous state of Zhou. In his territory, farmers united and grew produce in larger fields, and they also explored the deserted areas. They practiced fertilization and fire treatment for infestation. Their crops varied from rice and grains to beans. The government monopolized the trading of agricultural produce as well as slaves, animals, tools, and weapons. At that time, shells were the main currency and brass was starting to be put into practical use.

King Zhou Wen planned to declare war on King Shang Zhou. However, Zhou died before he was ready to do so. His ideals and thinking set the tone for the Zhou Dynasty and are the sources of Chinese Yi Jing and other Confucius works.

Below: King Zhou Wen with his mentor and adviser Jiangziya (left).

King Zhou Wu

(?–1043 BC)
Name: Ji Fa

Even though Zhou was far better developed than other areas in China at the time, tribes were still the basis of organization. After King Zhou Wu defeated King Shang Zhou, the Zhou Dynasty officially became a state—the Zhou Dynasty. King Zhou Wu divided the country into many regions and his relatives were granted lands, official titles, and regional authority. However, they had to report to the central government. Other rituals were also decided for the central court and regional states to follow.

Below: King Zhou Wu speaking to Shang civilians after overthrowing the Shang sovereign.

封諸侯

Above: King Zhou Wu started feudalism in China, and many of the 800 dukes who attended a conference he organized later joined him in attacking the Shang Dynasty forces, winning the Battle of Muye..

Left: King Zhou Wu set rituals for court.

King Zhou Cheng
(1042 BCñ1021 BC)
Name: Ji Yong

Prince of Zhou Wu, Ji Yong became a king at the age of thirteen. At the beginning of his reign it was in fact King Zhou Wu's brother Ji Dan who controlled the state. People often refer to him as Zhou Gong. During the process of merging with the previous Shang Dynasty, there were many Shang monarchal families. In order to easily manage them, rather than imprisoning or moving them to Zhouís central area, Zhou Gong decided to build them a new city and allowed them to stabilize themselves under the new Zhou sovereignty. The city was called Luoyi (today, Luoyang in Henan Province). Then they further developed the court regulations, rules, and rituals to affirm their central control.

Below: The young King Zhou Cheng being assisted by Zhou Gong.

Above: Zhou Gong, King Zhou Cheng's adviser.

Right: King Zhou Cheng sculpture in a shrine in Luoyang, Henan.

King Zhou You
(795 BC–771 BC)
Name: Ji Gongnie

King Zhou You was the 12th King of the Zhou Dynasty. According to historical records, there was an earthquake in the region in the second year of his reign. People superstitiously believed it forecast that the dynasty was about to come to an end. The following year, a beautiful lady, Baosi, came to the court as an empress. The king tried everything in his power to please Empress Baosi. First, he assigned Baosi's son as the heir apparent, canceling the crown prince title that had originally been granted to his son with his first wife. Baosi rarely smiled and in order to surprise her, King Zhou You had the idea of lighting the beacon fires, indicating that the capital was under attack. When the sub-state armies rushed to the capital, Baosi smiled. The same event was repeated a few times, frustrating leaders from the sub-states. When the state was really under attack by the barbarians from the western border, the king couldn't raise a defense. He was killed near the palace; the empress was nowhere to be found, and the dynasty ended.

Right: King You and Empress Baosi.

EASTERN ZHOU DYNASTY
(770 BC–256 BC)

King Zhou Ping
(781 BC–720 BC)
Name: Ji Yijiu

King Zhou Ping moved the capital from Haojing to Luoyi and named the dynasty the Eastern Zhou. Therefore historians named what was previously called Zhou the Western Zhou to distinguish between the two dynasties. The decline of the Zhou Dynasty and its central power weakened the Zhou imperial family. King Zhou Ping inherited the title as the leader but the sub-states no longer respected his authority. Without a solid military base controlled from the center, the regional monarchs developed to be much stronger and more independent.

Right: King Zhou Ping, son of King You of Zhou, first sovereign of the Eastern Zhou Dynasty, and thirteenth sovereign of the Zhou Dynasty. His posthumous name. Ping, means "peaceful."

Lord Qi Huan

(685 BC– 643 BC)
Name: Jiang Xiaobai

It is said that there were over forty monarchal states of the Zhou Dynasty, five of which were better developed than the others. They created a leadership circle and Lord Qi was the first executive. He separated the suburb from the city administration. Staffs were awarded according to the results of their work. He reduced taxes to increase the birth rate. There were also policies to even out food possession, therefore reducing the gap between rich and poor, and stabilizing society. His policy of providing basic life support to prisoners of war and widows attracted his neighboring country into wanting to move into Qi's territory.

Under his sovereignty, with the assistance of trusted politician Guan Zhong as prime minister, Qi region was far more developed compared to other countries in terms of economy, infrastructure, and population. Lord Qi died in a tragic staged coup. He was locked up in a cemetery for days and not until his rotten body was decomposing was he discovered.

Right: Under Lord Huan, Qi became the strongest state of the Spring and Autumn period.

Lord Song Xiang
(?–637 BC)
Name: Zi Cipu

State Song was not as strong as States Chu, Qin or Jin, although Lord Song Xiang was highly regarded among other states for his dignity, courteous manner, and generosity.

The Song and Chu met in battle at the Hongshui River in Southern China. While the Chu were crossing the river, the military adviser of Song was ready to strike the invader. However, Lord Song insisted on waiting for the Chu army to be fully ready for the battle after crossing the river. Ultimately Song lost the battle and Lord Song Xiang was injured during the war. He never recovered from his wounds and died the following year.

When Chong'er traveled to State Song during his exile, Lord Song, even under the pressure of Lord Jin, still treated him most diplomatically. Later, when the Chu were attacking Song and Jin, Lord Jin saved Song from falling after the Chengpu battle.

Right: Lord Song Xiang

Lord Qin Mu

(659 BC–621 BC)
Name: Ying Renhao

Some historical records recognize Qin Mu as one of the leaders of the circle, while others say he is well respected only in the west. Qin is located far west of other states. Distancing himself from other Zhou Dynasty's states, Lord Qin Mu was left out of the frequent disputes among other lords and monarchs. However, he was surrounded by barbarians in the west, who often threatened Qin's borders. The barbarians stole food and animals, and generally disturbed the normality of peoples' lives in that part of China.

Lord Qin cautiously allied those barbarian tribes, either with force or by diplomatic means, until he conquered the entire western territory (today, the Ning Xia and Gan Su Provinces). Such efforts built the foundation for Qin to conquer and unite China.

Left: Lord Qin Mu.

Lord Jin Wen
(697 BC–628 BC)
Name: Chong'er

Suspected of building a conspiracy with his brother, Shengshe, who was executed, Chong'er was exiled from Jin region. He was chased by his father, and tried to find place to survive. During this time he traveled to Qi, Song, Cao, Chu, Zheng, and Qin. Lord Chu took Chong'er under his wing, and to express his gratitude Chong'er promised that one day, if he controlled the army of Jin, he would back off ninety miles as a gift in return. Later Lord Qin married off his daughter to Chong'er and supported him in his return to Jin in order to become Lord Jin. Five years later, when Chu's army attacked Jin, Lord Jin Wen fulfilled his promise by pulling back his army by ninety miles. Still Lord Jin Wen defeated the Chu army, winning respect from the other states. He took the flagship of the leadership circle.

Right: Lord Jin Wen.

Lord Chu Zhuang

(?–591 BC)
Name: Xiong Minglv

At the beginning of the Zhou Dynasty, the Qi State had the largest territory, and most of the population, and was located in abundant and fruitful lands. When Lord Chu Zhuang was first enthroned, he indulged himself in the well-off life-style and ignored the administration. In the third year of his reign, Chancellor Wuju risked his life to explain and bring awareness to Lord Chu Zhuang that he could be valuable to his state. The story started with a bird: there was a giant bird resting in the state of Chu; it never flew nor made sound. One day the bird took off, flew so high and sung so loudly that it surprised everybody. The bird mirrored Lord Chu and by this metaphor urged that it was time for him to act since his state was expecting him to be a great leader.

Lord Chu felt ashamed and was motivated. He developed the economy of his own country, battled with the neighboring countries to boost the Chu's authority among other monarchal states, and finally allied the strongest states to build the leadership circle.

Below: Lord Chu Zhuang becoming leader of the leadership circle.

Right: Lord Chu Zhuang.

楚
莊
王

Lord Wu
(?–473 BC)
Name: Ji Fuchai

Lord Yue
(c. 520 BC–465 BC)
Name: Si Goujian

During the second year of his reign, Lord Wu defeated the Yue and imprisoned Lord Yue. When Lord Wu was ready to release Lord Yue to his home country, Counselor Wu Zixu was strongly against it. Not only did Lord Wu not appreciate the advice, but he executed Wu Zixu for opposing his decision.

Once Lord Yue returned to Yue, he immediately planned his revenge, and Lord Wu received a beautiful lady, Xi Shi, as a gift. Lord Wu was distracted from his main responsibilities. Some twenty years later, State Yue grew much stronger and launched an attack on Wu. Lord Wu escaped and later committed suicide.

In the second year of King Fuchai's reign, the Yue State was under attack and its forces were defeated. Lord Wu marched into the capital and took the surrendered Lord Yue prisoner. Humiliated, Lord Yue lived in Wu for three years under tough conditions and being forced to serve Fuchai. Three years later, Fuchai was touched by Lord Yue's obedience and released him.

Lord Yue of course, could not forget the humiliation he and his state bore. He focused on developing the economy and strengthening his military force. He finally defeated Lord Wu, totally dismantling the latter's sovereignty, and claimed his position in the leadership circle.

Left: Brass sword of Lord Wu inscribed (770 BC–476 BC).

Right: Brass spear of Lord Yue inscribed (475 BC–221 BC)

Lord Zhao Wuling
(340 BC–295 BC)
Name: Si Goujian

State Zhao was located between the Chinese territory and the northwestern Hu group who at the time were still barbaric. State Zhao was the first to construct long and high walls to protect its territory and borders. This is the original incarnation of the Great Wall of China. Later, many states learned this method of such a construction. Building the walls was very costly, however. It was an extraordinary expense for the state, and a labor-intensive project that required farmers to travel away from their lands, thus impacting on agricultural productivity.

One of the reasons for building high walls on hills to protect the borders was because the barbarians from the west and north were skilful horseback riders. Often the Chinese could not catch up with them. Lord Zhao Wuling decided to learn from the Hu group. He sent his troops to the plains near to the Hu's borders to learn and practice horseback riding and warfare. At home, domestic forces invented and produced new horse tackle and equipment.

In those days, local Chinese still wore long shirts, robes, and skirts with wide sleeves. In order to improve the mobility of the soldiers, Lord Zhao ordered his people to design new apparel in the Hu's style, such as wearing boots and tight-sleeved clothes. This revolutionary cultural adaptation greatly improved the domestic productivity as well as the soldiers' capabilities. The people of State Zhao, admiring the heroic figures and the great warrior spirit, enjoyed the reputation of favoring martial arts more than the rest of the country.

Left: Lord Zhao Wuling, whose people learned the art of horseback fighting, and more suitable battle dress, from the Hu.

Right: Illustration of the palace of Lord Zhao Wuling.

Lord Qin Xiao
(381 BC–338 BC)
Name: Ying Quliang

The name Warring State described the state of China when it was full of conflicts and war. But State Qin never played an important role until the very end of the period. Qin mainly dominated the west side of the country and, compared to the eastern states, it was considerably poorer. Its main industry was making brass works as well as clay crafts. When Lord Qin Xiao took over the reins of power, he publicly recruited people who could improve the country. Adviser Shang Yang answered the call. The famous Shang Yang Reform began and it was implemented with

the full authority of Lord Qin Xiao.

Shang Yang was a deep believer of strict laws to maintain social order—once law was instituted, everyone must obey. He abandoned the inheritance system in favor of attracting more talented people to serve in the court. Officials were expected to work hard in order to receive rewards such as title, land, and slaves. He also standardized units of measurement. Within Qin, the state was divided into counties for easier ruling. This series of alterations within the state built the foundation for the development of Qin throughout the country after the rest of the nation was conquered.

Left: Left: A brass jiang gu (domestic vessel) fom the household of Lord Qin Xiao.

Right: Right: Shang Yang was appointed adviser to Qin and immediately set about insituting strong laws and policy reforms for the good of the state. *(Fanghong)*

Following pages: The Battle of Chengpu, fought between the states of Jin against Chu and her advisers in 632 BC, during the Spring and Autumn Period, ending in a Jin victory.

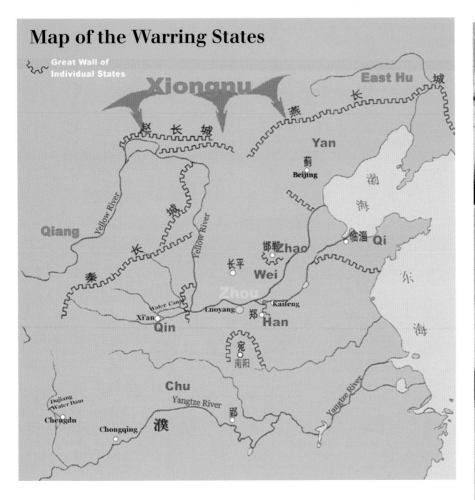

Map of the Warring States

Above: Map of the Warring States, a region in constant conflict.

Right: Lord Zhuang Xiang (right) and adviser Lv Buwei, a merchant who came to dominate the government and military of the Qin State.

QIN DYNASTY
(221 BC–206 BC)

Emperor Qin Shihuang (Qin, The First Emperor)

(221 BC–206 BC)
Name: Ying Zheng

Ying Zheng was crowned at the age of thirteen as leader of State Qin, celebrated his adulthood at twenty-one when he started to administer the state himself, and at thirty-nine finished a series of wars with other states by conquering them all and uniting China. This is when he changed his title to the Emperor Huang Di. In Chinese language Huang means imperial or power and Di means ruler. Leaders before his time were either called Huang or Di or King. Since he was the first to conquer all states and unite them as one country, to distinguish himself from previous leaders, he combined the two written characters into one

Right: Brass carriage found underground with the "terra-cotta armies."

phrase meaning "emperor." The "First" was also added in front of the title to show that what he did was unprecedented.

Thanks to him, China started to be seen as one country. The English word "China" was originally from Latin, the language of ancient Rome and the Roman Empire; Chin was how Qin had been pronounced. Unlike the way the Romans conquered, leaving the locals with some freedoms of living, Qin Shi Huang, once having eliminated the previous regime, would immediately switch the administration system to the Qin system in each state. This consistent and tight control helped to maintain his power as he proceeded to conquer the other states.

Before Qin, each state had its own forms of language, currency, and units of measurements. He ordered all states to follow the same system and launched one single currency across the nation—the round coin with square hole. Every six Chi was one Bu, and 240 Bu in a square was one Mu. This measurement system

was maintained for thousands of years. Even with roads, previously each state had its own style and measurement policy. When the emperor was traveling to the different countries, he found that his carts encountered difficulties in advancing due to the differences in road dimensions. So he ordered all roads to be standardized with one width—as wide as six Chi per cart. This greatly improved the transportation and thus communication among states.

Following the Qin State, he divided regions according to counties and within the counties there were towns. He appointed Prime Minister Li Si to investigate each state's written language and found Qi and Lu forms were more

easily written than others. The scholars combined the simplicity to the Qin written language and initiated one new written form. All other written languages were banned.

To erase other forms of writing script, Qin ordered older books to be destroyed, except those on medical and agricultural subjects useful for reference and adaptation. Confucians spoke openly, questioning the strictness of this legislation in comparison to the moderate governing from the Zhou Dynasty. When they protested against the burning of books, hoping to retain the classic literature, the emperor simply ordered them to be executed by burying them alive.

While he continued his expansion and control to unite China, the emperor also ordered his kingdom to be duplicated underground. To "preserve" his life-style after death, he constructed the underground palace on the outskirts of Xianyang (today, Xi'an) to imitate his living presence. Some eighteen miles away from downtown Xi'an at the presumed entrance of the emperor's tomb, gigantic terracotta army battalions, with as many as 8,000

Left: *Persecution of Confucians by Emperor Qin the First, with adviser Lv Buwei.*

figures, were discovered. What became known as the "terra-cotta armies" were sculpted with great detail and to human scale, standing or kneeling. They were arranged in formations as if they were ready for a battle.

Among many of the emperor's intensive projects one was to build the Great Wall. During the Warring State, many individual states had already built their own walls to obstruct the barbarians from the west or the north. But construction was costly. When the emperor united China, he decided to join all the western sides of the walls—so as to make them one wall to protect his vast kingdom. Every year, an estimated 400,000 farmers were drafted to the west for building the Great Wall; many never returned. Although the defense was breached numerous times, the Great Wall has since protected China from invasion from the west. Some parts of the original wall still remain but what visitors see today are mainly the re-installed sections from the Ming Dynasty.

Left: Life-size "terra-cotta warriors" found near the Qin tomb.

Emperor Qin Er'shi (Qin, The Second Emperor)

(259 BC–207 BC)
Name: Ying Hugai

Ying Hugai was the twenty-sixth son of the first emperor. He took over the reign with the assistance of Prime Mister Li Si. But the reign didn't come so easily. Domestically, Ying Hugai had to murder his brother, and politically the Qin's ruling was challenged by rebellions. The country was falling apart due to many years of war, lavish projects like the First Emperor's tomb and the Great Wall, and the tyranny of the First Emperor. Qin Er'shi, after conducting a nationwide inspection, decided to tighten the laws still further. However, the laws were too strict to follow and were unfavorable to the peasants. The year after he was crowned, Li Si conspired in the suicide of Ying Hugai.

Right: A performance at the Qin tomb to represent a memorial of an emperor during the Qin Dynasty.

WESTERN HAN DYNASTY
(202 BC–9 AD)

Emperor Han Gao

(256 BC–195 BC)
Name: Liu Bang
Memorial name: Han Tai Zu, Gaozu

Liu Bang was one of the most successful rebellion leaders during the movement to overturn the ruling from the Qin Dynasty. After defeating his only strong opponent, he established Han Dynasty.

He continued much of the Qin system and bureaucracies but the key was to revise the imperious laws and tyrannical punishments. On the basis of Qin Law, he

Left: The character "gate" embossed on a clay tile from Hangu Gate.

Above: Liu Bang, first emperor of the Han Dynasty.

revised Nine Section Han Law and added residence identification regulation, marriage law, and taxation according an individual's status in the society. Han Twelve Volume Ritual was also instituted. He reintroduced Confucius thinking—to rule the country with a moderate attitude but enforced by the written law.

The Han administration attracted many formerly remote people to establish residences in the middle of the country, boosting the economy. Liu Bang's policies were continued for over 400 years by the Han Dynasty and by generations that followed. Some historians consider Liu Bang as the great leader who united China, as Han China, who established Han culture as one system. Therefore, the majority of the Chinese are called Han Chinese.

Above: Luo Yang, Henan Province—a key geographical position for Liu Bang during the rebellion.

Left: Detail of showing the royal entourage in the mountains from "The First Emperor of the Han Dynasty Entering Kuan Tung" by Chao Po-chu. (*Burstein Collection/Corbis BE005956*)

Emperor Han Wudi
(156 BC –87 BC)
Name: Liu Che
Memorial name: Han Shizong

Liu Che was the fifth emperor of the Han Dynasty. The influences of his sovereignty reached mid-Asia, Chinese Dongbei, Hainan, and all over the east coast. He initiated many more systems, policies, and regulations than Liu Bang and Qin Shihuang, considered "the first" in Chinese history.

For example, the first written archive of Chinese history was by his historian chancellor; it was named "Records of the Grand Historian" (Shi Ji). In it, borders of the state were marked on paper as maps to outline the territory. He designed the public examination system to call up capable people for serving at court. To understand the western neighbors, Zhang Qian was sent to the West for diplomatic missions. His was the beginning of the Silk Road connecting East to the West.

One of the most important decisions was to declare Confucius as the principal thinking for the state. This policy lasted till the end of the imperialism at the ebb of the Qing Dynasty.

Liu Che fell ill in 88 BC without an heir apparent. He chose his youngest son, who was only six years old, to inherit his throne with the support of Huo Gang. His reign lasted for fifty-four years, making him one of the longest ruling emperors in history. This record was not broken until 1800 years later, by Emperor Kang Xi from the Qing Dynasty.

Above: Su Wu, an ambassador of Emperor Han Wu to Xiognu, was kept hostage for nineteen years. When he returned to Han he found that Han Wu had died and it was now Han Shao's reign.

Emperor Han Shao

(94 BC–74 BC)
Name: Liu Fuling
Memorial name: Han Xiaoshao

Liu Fuling was Emperor Han Wu's most favorite son. He was made heir-apparent and enthroned at only thirteen years of age. Before Emperor Han Wu died, he was worried that Liu Fuling's youth and innocence would be taken advantage of by his mother or some officials in order to

Left: Mural painting found in the Han Dynasty tomb. It reveals how well-off people traveled.

grasp authority. Therefore Emperor Han Wu executed his mother and appointed two trustees to endorse the junior emperor.

The administration simply inherited everything from the previous administration. As Liu Fuling grew older and more experienced, he made moderate changes to what his father had designed, such as shifting the military strategy from attack to defense in order to retain peace with the western barbarians, and proposing settlement by marriage with the western leaders.

XIN DYNASTY
(8–23 AD)

Emperor Xin Yuan
(45 BC–23 AD)
Name: Wang Mang
Memorial name: None

In the first official overthrow of an emperor in Chinese history, the last emperor of the Han Dynasty resigned, handing the sovereignty to Wang Mang.

Wang Mang was a creative politician. He insisted on reforms in the military, society, and economy of the Han Dynasty. However, Han sovereignty was already deeply rooted in the peoples' minds. His currency innovation to create three kinds of coins at the same time was not well understood, causing inflation. With several natural disasters adding to the pressure, a number of rebels sprouted to revert back the Han Dynasty. In 23 AD, the rebels marched into the capital Chang'an (today, Xi'an) and Wang Mang was murdered by a merchant.

Right: Wang Mang, one-time regent for Emperor Ping, ascended to the throne in 9 AD.

EASTERN HAN DYNASTY
(25–220)

Emperor Han Guangwu

(5 BC–57 AD)
Name: Liu Xiu
Memorial name: Han Shizu

Liu Xiu led the rebellion of 8,000 people to meet Wang Mang's troops in Kungyang. Although he was outnumbered, he defeated Wang Mang and dismantled the Xin sovereignty. Liu Xiu's courage and bravery in the face of a superior power, and the ability to turn a situation to his favor, won him respect among the people. He re-established the Han Dynasty, called Eastern Han.

His sovereignty was also called Guangwu Prosperity. His moderate policies built a solid foundation from which his dynasty could advance further. Under his rule, slaves received some rights of their own, the penalties for committing crime were downgraded, and taxes were reduced.

Left: A coin from the Eastern Han period.

Right: Emperor Han Guangwu, founder of the Eastern Han Dynasty.

Right: Emperor Guangwu (Liu Xiu) He was founder of the Later Han or Eastern Han, ruling parts of China at first, then the whole of China after suppression of regional warlords and defeating his many rivals for the throne, in particular the peasant army of the Chimei. Although he gained the throne by force of arms, as emperor he was considered a man of peace and mercy who introduced reforms (mainly regarding land and society) that stood the Han Dynasty in good stead for 200 years. This is Han Guangwu's gravestone. He was succeeded by Crown Prince Zhuang, who ascended the throne as Emperor Ming.

Left: A mythical creature stands guard over the grave of Emperor Han Guangwu.

Far right: Border protection has always been important to Chinese emperors. This is a model of a watchtower from the Han Dynasty. (*Royal Ontario Museum/Corbis RM001072*)

Emperor Han Shao

(176–190)
Name: Liu Bian
Memorial name: Nong Huai

Liu Bian was the twelfth emperor of the Eastern Han Dynasty. When his father was very ill Liu Bian was appointed the next emperor at age thirteen, over his brother Liu Xie. The young emperor didn't have the power to resist conflict within the court, and was kidnapped and forced to commit suicide. He was only eighteen years old.

Right: Emperor Han Shao, whose name means "young emperor."

Emperor Han Xian

(181–234)
Name: Liu Xie

When Emperor Han Shao's father died, warlord Dong Zhuo increased his power by taking control of the military forces. He installed Liu Bian's younger brother Liu Xie to the throne as a puppet emperor in order to be above all other regional leaders. For the same reason, after Dong Zhuo died, Cao Cao moved Liu Xie to Xu Chang and recapitalized there. Cao Cao's son later pressed Liu Xie to resign, ending the Han Dynasty.

Historical records describe Liu Xie, a child emperor whose authority was never established, as having a moderate and mild personality. In 214, Liu Xie saw civilians were suffering from starvation due to a few serious natural disasters. He requested that the royal warehouses offer rice congee for the refugees, and also punished the officials who were taking advantage and stealing from the state storage. He was only fourteen years of age.

Right: Emperor Han Xian, author of "The Literary Mind and the Carving of Dragons," China's first work of aesthetics and literary criticism.

THE THREE KINGDOMS: WEI, SHU, WU
(184–280)

Emperor Wei Wu

(155–220)
Name: Cao Cao
Memorial name: Wei Taizu

Cao Cao was a multi-talented leader, well respected by his opponents during the Three Kingdom period. He established Kingdom Wei, dominating Northern China, with a population of 4.5 million. After Dong Zhuo died, Cao Cao seized the military, and continued to hold Emperor Han Xian hostage while battling with other states at the same time, with the aim of conquering the rest of China. He believed in reforms and created the idea of multi-tasking his army—during times of peace, soldiers were to perform civil service by helping in the fields. This policy greatly improved the agricultural productivity and eased the starvation rampant in his kingdom, caused by wars and disasters.

A poet himself, he emphasized education within the family. The Cao family left behind many classic poems and songs. He also drew talented poets to his side and

Below: Cao Cao's son Cao Shi's poems inspired this scroll painting.

Left: One of the central figures of the Three Kingdoms period, Cao Cao was considered a harsh disciplinarian who laid the foundations of the Wei Kingdom.

Above: Cao Cao composing a poem. He and his sons Cao Pi and Cao Zhi are credited with reshaping the poetry style of their time.

established the Jian'an Poet Community. To track the literature history, every poet from that time was connected with Cao Cao. During the turmoil of the Three Kingdoms situation, Chinese written and spoken language advanced and many historians attribute this achievement to Cao Cao. On the one hand, he recruited talented people to join his administration. On the other hand, many people who answered his call were executed some time later due to minor errors. He was said to be a great and talented leader who had a bad temper and jealous personality.

Above: Cao Cao with (kneeling) Lui Bei, a general, warlord, and later founding emperor of Shu Han during the Three Kingdoms era.

Ambitious as he was, Cao Cao never titled himself as emperor but as the King of Wei. It was his son, after his death, who announced the establishment of the Wei Dynasty and brought an end to the Han Dynasty by forcing Emperor Han Xian to resign, and enthroning himself as an emperor. His son reconciled Cao Cao's success with a memorial name Wei Taizu (The Great Ancestor of Wei).

Cao Pi inherited his father's passion for literary art, opened a state school, and instituted a doctorate degree for graduates. Perhaps his successes were not comparable to those of his father, but many of his policies continued the development of society, boosted the economy, and allowed him to grasp control of his sovereignty.

The tight control also extended to his competitive brothers. During his short reign of six years, he tried every means to obstruct his brothers from being near to any authority.

A classic poem written by Cao Zhi, Cao Pi's younger brother, proved his viciousness. Cao Pi was jealous of Cao Zhi's talent and found justification to have him burned at the stake. He ordered Cao Zhi to create a poem within seven steps while walking to his death. Cao Zhi walked towards the fire tearfully and recited this poem named "The Seven Steps":

Cooked are the beans,
As their stalks feed the fire,
Beans weep, stalks expire,
Same root we grew,
Why treat each other so cruel?
(Translation by Ma Yan)

In this poem, Cao Zhi used the beans and stalks coming from the same plant as a metaphor for himself and his brother. People usually harvest the beans and use their stems to fuel the fire during cooking—both will be consumed. Through this poem, Cao Zhi was asking his brother to think carefully: as brothers they were from the same mother and father, and (when the state could be attacked any time} why should they kill each other?

Cao Pi wept after hearing the poem and released his brother to live in a remote area far from his administration.

Emperor Wei Wen

(187–226)
Name: Cao Pi
Memorial name: Wei Shizu

Cao Cao had sixteen wives and twenty-five sons. Many were talented and well educated. Every one of them was a poet and some produced masterpieces. Cao Pi was among the most competitive. After hesitating for many years, at his deathbed Cao Cao passed his throne to Cao Pi.

Emperor Wei Ming

(205–239)
Name: Cao Rui

Another poet from the Cao family, Cao Rui naturally continued the literary policies of his father Cao Pi and grandfather Cao Cao. Furthermore, he employed people to research and study poems and the Chinese language. Later he, Cao Pi, and Cao Cao were named the Three Masters (of poetry). Their poems and essays were re-edited and published during the Qing Dynasty.

Cao Rui's reign lasted thirteen years, during which time he streamlined the penalty laws from the Qin and Han Dynasties. He also had some military successes against Kingdoms Shu and Wu. After the military adviser Zhuge Liang from Shu died, Cao Rui coud see the triangle of equilibrium was broken and provoked more wars, as well as building his luxurious palace. At the end of his life, Kingdom Wei was close to bankruptcy.

Right: Emperor Wei Ming (Cao Rui) spent heavily on palace building and ancestral temples.

Emperor Wei Jingyuan

(246–302)
Name: Cao Huan
Memorial name: Wei Yuandi

Inheriting the title Emperor of Wei at the age of fourteen, Cao Huan became one of many puppet emperors in Chinese history. In 265 Sima Yan, chancellor of Cao Huan, disclaimed his title and offered to move Cao Huan to Yecheng and for him to be titled King of Chenliu as a reminder of the Wei Dynasty. The Wei Dynasty ended when Cao Huan was forced to abdicate in favor of Sima Yan, establishing the Jin Dynasty.

Right: Cao Huan, last emperor of Cao Wei during the Three Kingdoms period.

Emperor Shu

(181–234)
Name: Liu Bei, Liu Xuande
Memorial name: Shu Zhaoliedi

Liu Bei was a descendant of Emperor Han Jing from the Eastern Han Dynasty. However, he was born poor and made a living by selling bamboo sheets with his mother. During a rebellion, Liu Bei met his soul mates Guan Yu and Zhang Fei. They swore to be blood brothers. Later, with the assistance of the political and military adviser Zhuge Liang, he gathered forces of his own and declared the independence of State Shu. At that time, States Wei and Wu were already two stable states. Liu Bei's policies attracted residents to move into his region, thus expanding it to a stable state and boosting the economy. His declaration of independence marked the beginning of China in a triangle of equilibrium with three states.

Without Zhuge Liang's help, Liu Bei could have fought

Below: Liu Bei (at rear) with blood brothers Guan Yu and Zhang Fei.

Above: Liu Bei (right) on one of the three journeys he made to Zhuge Liang to invite him to act as adviser at court.

Left: Zhang Fei made a crucial error in the Battle of Xuzhao, and asked Liu Bei (in yellow) to execute him.

in vain against two other states. But his story of inviting Zhuge Liang won him respect due to his humble and patient character. His advisers Xu Shu and Sima Hui recommended that he invite Zhuge Liang into giving up his idyllic life in the mountains and assisting him in court.

It was a long journey into the mountains, and Liu Bei visited three times before he could meet Zhuge Liang in person. During their meeting, Zhuge Liang was content with Liu Bei's humble character and expressed his opinions as to how Liu Bei could build a state while Wei

and Shu were already very established. After that, Liu Bei respected Zhuge Liang as his teacher until his last days, when he committed Zhuge Liang to assist his son in continuing his dream.

Above: *Zhang Fei and Ma Chao during the Battle of Xiamenguan. After suffering defeat, Ma Chao joined Lui Bei's campaign.*

Emperor Shu Houzhu
(181–234)
Name: Liu Shan

Liu Shan was seventeen when his father Liu Bei died. Liu Bei had begged Zhuge Liang to help the young emperor in all state affairs. For eleven years, Zhuge Liang and Liu Shan worked together to administer State Shu. As Liu Shan grew older and more experienced, however, there were disagreements between the two. In the eleventh year of his reign, Zhuge Liang died. Having been antagonized by him for so many years, Liu Shan banned the role and title of prime mister in Shu, which Zhuge Liang had held for decades. He divided the prime mister's role into three: the commander in chief, the chancellor, and the judge. Unfortunately, he lost control of them and the administration fell apart. Unable to defend himself, in 263 he surrendered to Wei and drew State Shu to an end. He was relocated to Luoyang and lived comfortably. As he said himself, "I don't miss my country at all."

Right: Liu Shan, second and last emperor of the Kingdom of Shu during the Three Kingdoms period.

Emperor Wu

(182–252)
Name: Sun Quan
Memorial name:
The Great Emperor of Wu

State Wu was also called Eastern Wu since it was located in Eastern China. Sun Quan inherited the leadership from his brother, Sun Ce. To curb Cao Cao's development in State Wei, he supported Liu Bei in his early years. In Chibi, he formed an alliance with Liu Bei to fight against Cao Cao, who was defeated and greatly weakened after this battle. When Cao Pi claimed independence and established Wei as a kingdom, Sun Quan first joined his court and swore to obey his leadership, but later declared his own title as an emperor of Wu.

Wu was first capitalized in Jianye (modern-day Nanjing) in 211; then the capital was moved to Wuchang. The same year that Sun Quan declared Wu as an independent state, in 229, he moved the administration back to Jianye, satisfied that it was a convenient location for trading, and transportation, as well as a key position in which to hold his military force.

Right: An imperious statue of Sun Quan, founder of Eastern Wu during the Three Kingdoms period.

Emperor Wu Jing
(235–264)
Name: Sun Xiu

Sun Xiu was the sixth son of Sun Quan. In contrast with other leaders born in that period, Sun Xiu lacked the martial instinct. He took over the crown from his brother with reluctance, and lost nearly every war he fought. At home, he implemented policies in favor of growing the economy and promoting Confucianism.

Right: The young emperor Sun Xiu conspired with his advisers to have regent Sun Lin captured and executed for fear of being overthrown by him.

WESTERN JIN AND EASTERN JIN
(265–316)   *(317–420)*

Emperor Xuan Wang

(179–251)
Name: Sima Yi
Memorial name: Jin Xuandi

Sima Yi originally served in the Wei court. He won the trust of the Cao family because of his early endorsement of Cao Cao to establish Wei. For Cao Cao's offsprings, however, he was in a key position to assist the Wei emperors to develop the country, but did the opposite. When Cao Pi died, Sima Yi was appointed as the prime minister and custodian, assisting Cao Rui. The Sima family took advantage of their prime position to work through the administration to assemble their power. When Cao Rui died in 240 Sima Yi was asked to assist the successor, Cao Fang, which he did. At no time during his reign did Cao Fang have real authority, which was essentially held by Sima Yi. In 249, Sima Yi overthrew the Wei sovereignty in a coup during the Wei emperor's absence from court. He took over the army and prepared to establish his own dynasty.

Like many other leaders during the Three Kingdoms period, Sima Yi encouraged laws to increase agricultural productivity. He embraced Cao Cao's idea of utilizing military manpower in the gaps between wars, for cultivating the fields. He expanded the scale of those fields, and moved the food reserves closer to the central government in order to ensure sufficient supply for government and military use.

Sima Yi died before the Jin Dynasty was established. His son Sima Zhao continued his dream and honored him with the memorial name Jin Gaozu.

Below: Sima Yi defended .Cao Wei against the Zhuge Liang Northern Expeditions during the Three Kingdoms era.

Emperor Jin Wu

(236–290)
Name: Sima Yan
Memorial name: Jin Shizu

To finish the ambitions his father, Sima Zhao, left behind, Sima Yan established the Jin Dynasty in 265. At the beginning of Sima Yan's administration, Jin steadily developed, due to the foundations his father and uncles had built. By the end of the Three Kingdoms period, civilians were tired of war and instability. The economy slowed down and people in many areas were suffering starvation. He instituted the social hierarchy according to people's productivity, then divided the fields according to their productivity hierarchy. Taxes were also levied according to this social system. This policy temporarily stimulated people's trust in the administration and encouraged growth of the economy.

However, in contrast with other fledgling emperors in history, Sima Yan indulged himself in a lavish lifestyle. In 289, he became ill and died soon after, leaving his crown to a retarded son. A seed of instability grew within the dynasty that his father and uncles had devoted their lives to build. The Jin Dynasty terminated only twenty-five years after his death.

Above: Sima Yan was the first emperor of the Jin Dynasty.

Right: Emperor Jin Wu and attendants. Detail of "Portraits of Thirteen Emperors attributed to Yen Li-pen. *(Burstein Collection/Corbis)*

晉武帝司馬炎

Emperor Jin Yuan

(276–522)
Name: Sima Rui
Memorial name: Jin Zhongzong

The Xiongnu were thought to be primitive tribes of the early Turkish and Mongolian clans. Xiongnu was the name given by the Han Chinese. They had been threatening and disturbing Chinese western borders since eras before the Qin dynasty, and were considered as barbarians compared to the ancient Chinese civilization. Qin, the First Emperor, joined the defensive walls in the west to prevent the Xiongnu from invading, and all other dynasties continued this work, as well as sacrificing female courtiers into marriage with Xiongnu in exchange for peace. During the Three Kingdoms period, the Chinese were more involved with their power fight to rule China than paying attention to the Xiongnu tribes, who advanced themselves by learning Chinese culture.

In 316, the first time in history for such an action, the Jin Dynasty was overthrown by the Xiongnu tribes. Sima Rui, a descendant from the Sima bloodline, escaped to the south. In Jiankang (today, Nanjing), he re-established the "Jin" Dynasty, usually referred to as the Eastern Jin. The dynasty, without a strong military force, wobbled through a hundred years of rule, assisted by the Chinese, who were not willing to obey the Xiongnu tribes. Sima Rui died in 323

after an illness caused by injuries received when he lost a regional battle in Wuchang.

Above: Sima Rui was emperor of the Jin Dynasty, and first emperor of the Eastern Jin Dynasty.

FIVE HUS AND SIXTEEN KINGDOMS
(304–439)

Emperor of Western Liang
(351–417)
Name: Li Hao
Memorial name: Liang Wu Zhaowang

Located in Jiuquan (modern-day Gansu Province), the Western Liang was one of the empires ruled by the Chinese. There were three emperors who ruled this region for twenty-two years. Li Hao, who established it, was the first. Since he was a serious reader, his policies were oriented around education and promoting literature. These policies attracted many intellectuals to take residence in his region. Together there were many academic achievements. Li Hao himself wrote many articles for scholars to study, but very few were preserved.

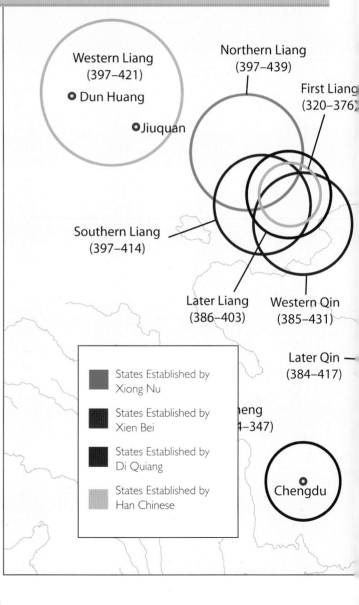

Western Liang
(397–421)

○ Dun Huang

○Jiuquan

Northern Liang
(397–439)

First Liang
(320–376)

Southern Liang
(397–414)

Later Liang
(386–403)

Western Qin
(385–431)

Later Qin —
(384–417)

...eng
...4–347)

Chengdu

States Established by
Xiong Nu

States Established by
Xien Bei

States Established by
Di Quiang

States Established by
Han Chinese

Right: The map reflects a period of more than 130 years.

Map of Five Hus and Sixteen Kingdoms

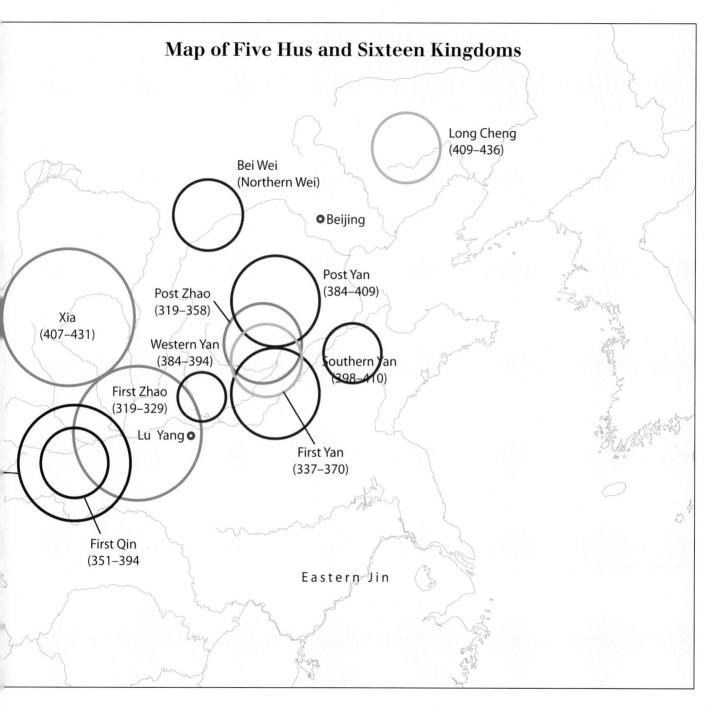

Long Cheng
(409–436)

Bei Wei
(Northern Wei)

⊙Beijing

Post Yan
(384–409)

Post Zhao
(319–358)

Xia
(407–431)

Western Yan
(384–394)

Southern Yan
(398–410)

First Zhao
(319–329)

Lu Yang ⊙

First Yan
(337–370)

First Qin
(351–394

Eastern Jin

SOUTHERN DYNASTIES:
Song, Qi Liang, Chen
(420–589)

Eastern Wei:
Emperor Wei Xiaojing

(524–551)
Name: Yuan Shanjian

Emperor Wei Xiaowu was afraid of Lord Gao Huan's dominance, and escaped from it. Gao Huan enthroned eleven-year-old Yuan Shanjian as Emperor Wei Xiaojing. A puppet emperor, Yuan Shanjian was terrified by Gao Huan throughout his life. After Gao Huan died, he was murdered by Gao Huan's grandson, who started Empire Qi to end Eastern Wei.

Emperor Xiaojing grew to be handsome and strong young man, capable of jumping over a fence while holding a stone lion. He was also said to be skillful at horse riding, archery, and literature. People compared him to his famed ancestor, Emperor Xiaowen.

But life was not pleasant for the young emperor. Actual authority rested in the hands of Gao and other officials that Gao delegated authority to. In 536, Gao put his son Gao Cheng in charge of the Eastern Wei government. Late that year, Emperor Xiaojing's father Yuan Dan died, amid suggestions that he was assassinated on the orders of Gao Huan.

In 544, Gao Cheng, wanting to install a trusted official to keep watch on Emperor Xiaojing, placed his associate

Cui Jishu as Emperor Xiaojing's secretary. In 547, Gao Huan died, and Gao Cheng took over full power of the government. Emperor Xiaojing joined in a conspiracy to overthrow Gao Cheng, but this was discovered, and the emperor was arrested and put under house arrest.

In spring 549, Emperor Xiaojing was forced to offer Gao Cheng the greater title of Prince of Qi, and also the

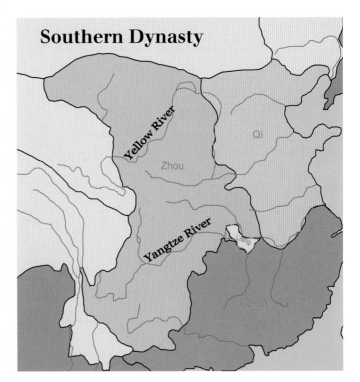

Southern Dynasty

honorific office of Xiangguo, signaling a move toward Gao's taking of the throne. While formally declining these offers, Gao Cheng was planning with others the timetable for taking the throne. But Gao Cheng was himself assassinated, and his brother, Gao Yang, quickly moved to consolidate power, forcing the emperor to abdicate in favor of a new emperor, Wenxuan. The latter, always concerned that Emperor Xiaojing would move to usurp him, sent assassins to force the former emperor to drink poisoned wine, and also killed his three sons. Emperor Wenxuan gave the former emperor the posthumous name of Xiaojing, and also buried him with imperial honors.

Emperor Chen Wen

(552–566)
Name: Chen Xi
Memorial name: Chen Shizu

Chen Xi was the second emperor of the Chen Dynasty. During his reign of seven years, he focused on leading the country with agricultural

Left: Southern Dynasty, from the establishment of Chen in 420, including Chen, Song, Qi, and Liang Dynasties.

development instead of martial movements. Domestically, a scandal involving him attracted historians' attention. He was said to feel affection for Han Zigao, a good-looking shoemaker, and made an attempt to start a relationship with him. The request for forming a liaison between the two didn't succeed; had it done so, the Chen Dynasty could have produced the first "male" empress in history!

Emperor Chen Fei

(554–570)
Name: Chen Bozong

Chen Bozong was the son of Chen Xi. He inherited the throne at eleven years of age. It was his uncle who looked after the administration. His advisers pushed his mother to void his title within two years and to have him transferred to a remote residence.

Emperor Chen Xuan

(530–568)
Name: Chen Xu

Chen Xu was originally the chancellor for Chen Bozong. Two years later he inaugurated himself, naming his era Taijian. Besides developing his own

state, Chen Xu battled with both States Qi and Zhou. While he succeeded with Qi, the loss to Zhou later proved to be deadly for the State of Chen.

Emperor Chen Houzhu

(553–604)
Name: Chen Shubao

After his father Chen Xu died, the reign was left officially to Chen Shubao. During the funeral, his younger brother Chen Shuling attempted to kill him to steal the reign, but didn't succeed. Within a short period of time after inauguration, Chen Shubao collected seventeen empresses in the palace. The big project of rebuilding the palace also started right away. Chen Shubao was said to be a very talented poet, but not so good at administering the country. In 581, State Zhou was diminished by Yang Jian, who established the Sui Dynasty. Chen Shubao did not feel any threat of what happened to his neighboring country, thinking that the Sui army would never cross the Yangtze River. In 588, the Sui did cross and reached Jiankang (today, Nanjing). Chen was ended. Chen Shubao was found hiding in a well.

NORTHERN DYNASTIES:
Bei Wei, Bei Qi, Bei Zhou, and more
(386–581)

Northern Wei
Emperor Wei Xiaowen

(467–499)
Name: Tuoba Hong (Yuan Hong)
Memorial name: Wei Gaozu

The Northern Wei Dynasty was a state ruled by Xianbei, one of the ethnic groups in China. Tuoba Hong inherited the throne when he was five years old. By the time, he grew up he continued the reforms that had been started by his grandmother, Empress Feng, although he was more courageous and radical about trying new things. His mother was Chinese and many of his policies were to encourage Xianbei people to communicate with the Chinese and integrate the two cultures. His series of reforms were intended to make the Xianbei people develop, following Chinese examples. They were encouraged to wear Han attire, speak and write Han Chinese, and marry Chinese people. At the same time he introduced Buddhism to the Chinese, which immediately became popular.

Right and far right: There are more than 100,000 statues in the Longmen Grottoes, one of the three most famous ancient sculptural sites in China (the others being the Mogao Caves and the Yungang Grottoes). Approximately one-third of the caves date from the Northern Wei Dynasty.

Emperor Wei Xuanwu

(483–515)
Name: Tuoba Ke (Yuan Ke)
Memorial name: Wei Shizong

The second son of Emperor Wei Xiaowen, Tuoba became the emperor at the age of sixteen. He continued the policies set out by his father, and it was during his reign that the Northern Wei Dynasty and city of Luoyang reached their prime.

Left: A guard at Tuoba Ke's tomb, now open to the public as part of the Luoyang Ancient Tombs Museum.

Above: The coffin of Tuoba Ke, who died suddenly in 515.

NORTHERN ZHOU DYNASTIES
(507–556)

Emperor Wu
(543–578)
Name: Yuwen Yi

Yuwen Yi was the third emperor of Zhou. During his reign he was very enthusiastic for Xianbei people to learn Chinese culture. He lived and managed his reign in favor of the Chinese structure too. One of the most significant policies was to confirm that Chinese Confucianism was the principal religion of his administration, Daoism being the second, and Buddhism only third. The following year, he even banned both Buddhism and Daoism in his state, and monks were requested to give up their religion to return to their original homes. Yuwen Yi attacked Qi three times and finally managed to overthrow the Qi administration. His success in marginalizing Qi made it easy for Yangjian to unite China again and establish the Sui Dynasty.

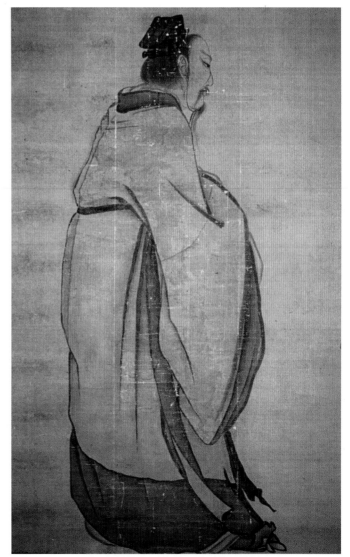

Right: Early in his reign, Yewen Yi was dominated by his cousin Yewen Hu, but he seized power and in 572 ambushed Yewen Hu, so that he could rule capably. *(The Art Archive/National Palace Museum Taiwan AA335589)*

SUI DYNASTY
(581–618)

Emperor Sui Wen

(541–604)
Name: Yang Jian
Memorial name: Sui Gaozu

After over 400 years of separation and wars since the Eastern Han Dynasty, Yang Jian unified China again. Learning lessons from the previous dynasty, the bureaucratic system was streamlined. Following the Sui Dynasty, China was rarely divided again.

Between the Jin Dynasty and the beginning of Sui Dynasty, various states and dynasties were carrying out similar policies: promoting Chinese culture and building Xianbei armies. Yet there were still social discriminations between the two groups. After the Sui Dynasty was established, Yang Jian immediately conducted a national census to gain a head count and set the taxation accordingly.

He saved the Han Chinese culture by collecting rare books that survived after many wars, such that several books from as early as the Han Dynasty were preserved. Under his sovereignty, the population grew, food productivity increased, and China became more peaceful and stable again. This period is appraised as the "Beginning Era of Prosperous."

Right: Terra-cotta figure from the Sui Dynasty. *(The Art Archive/National Palace Museum Taiwan AA363919)*

Emperor Sui Yang

(569–618)
Name: Yang Guang
Memorial name: Sui Shizu

Yang Guang was often compared to emperors Shang Zhou and Qin First Emperor for his cruelty and tyranny. However, one of his great successes was the 1,114-mile-long Grand Canal in eastern China. The idea was initiated originally as a convenience for Yang Guang himself. It was then extended to enable agricultural produce to be sent to the North. The canal was a costly project to begin with, and the expense increased tax pressure on the civilians, drawing wide criticism later since the outlay for his lavish travels was beyond his means.

The Emperor Sui Yang was an artist and art collector. He ordered all the palace book collections to be duplicated to conserve the archives, compositions and art pieces. To show off these treasures, among many others, he insisted on increasing diplomatic communications with the western regions, while their merchants were also offered benefits if they were visiting China for trading. For instance, the Chinese traders were forced to offer free dining and accommodations.

Perhaps because of the wars against Korea that he lost, and the cost of maintaining his extravagant life-style, much political pressure was built up. To relieve himself of the heavy burden of administration, he became an alcoholic. The rebellion of his trustees, led by Yuwen Hua, overran the capital, and Yang Guang was sentenced to death.

Above: Yang Guang's name was originally Yang Ying, but his father, Emperor Sui Wen, changed it after consulting with oracles. It has been suggested that Yang Guang was implicated in the murder of his father in 604. This is an 18th Century depiction of him on his boat on the Grand Canal. *(The Art Archive /Bibliothèque Nationale Paris)*

TANG DYNASTY
(618–907)

Emperor Tang Wude
(566–635)
Name: Li Yuan
Memorial name: Tang Gaozu

Li Yuan was a cousin of Yang Guang, the last emperor of Sui. They both had Xianbei mothers but were brought up in the way of the Chinese. Yang Guang trusted Li Yuan to command part of the army, since he had defeated Tujue (another western tribe) as well as having quashed some minor regional rebellions. Approaching the end of the Sui Dynasty, more and more farmers rebelled against Yang Guang's administration, and Li Yuan joined the opposition. In 617, his troops marched into Chang'an and started the Tang Dynasty.

To begin his sovereignty, Li Yuan continued similar policies from the Sui but discontinued the arbitrary taxes disliked by the civilians. Then the Sui Laws were modified to the Tang Laws. The few alterations stabilized the society and built a sound base for the rest of the dynasty, especially for Li Yuan's son, Li Shimin, who ruled after him.

There were many conflicts and disputes regarding his heir. Rivalry among his sons brought serious problems to the home. In 622, Li Shimin ambushed his brother at the gate of the capital, Gate Xuanwu, and held his father hostage. Li Yuan was forced to make Li Shimin the heir-apparent and to retire shortly after. Li Yuan was promoted to Supreme Emperor for his retirement. He lived away from the palace, and died of illness in 635.

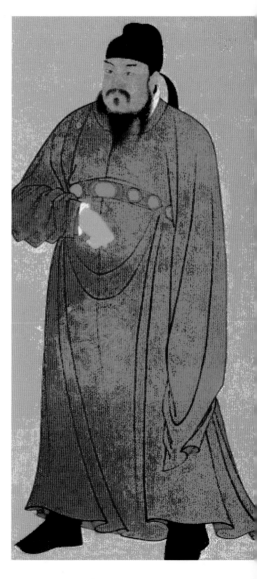

Right: Li Yuan established the Tang Dynasty as Emperor Tang Wude (also Emperor Gaozu) in 618, and set about attempting to unite the empire.

Emperor Tang Zhenguan

(599–649)
Name: Li Shimin
Memorial name: Tang Taizong

Except for his abrupt action against his father and brothers to seize control of the throne, Li Shimin has been considered the perfect model leader in history, his achievements bringing about the peak of prosperity to China, called "Reign of Zhen'guan." More often referred to by his memorial name.

Li Shimin was a liberal thinker and leader. He opened up the border controls and ports to allow trading. Many foreigners moved into Chang'an (modern-day Xi'an) to live. Communication with many countries was increased. Li Shimin encouraged foreigners to visit and learn about Chinese culture, and even the Chinese language. It was the first time in history that embassies were established to help foreign students live in Chang'an. After visits to Tang by their representatives, Japan and Korea, for example, carried out reforms throughout their countries so as to input the Chinese political system and educate their people to live in the Chinese style. The Silk Road prospered and connected East and West in terms of culture as well as trade, and was seen as the "golden pavement" by merchants.

During Li Shimin's reign, corruption was rare, society suffered little crime, and even if errors were made, the punishment was minor. The main method of changing people was through education. Li Shimin himself set a good example to his administrators. He invited his advisers to regularly point out his wrongdoings and would make amends whenever he could. His humility has been appreciated by later emperors, and advocated as the essential virtue of leadership even today.

Literature was one of his favorite subjects, as well as calligraphy. During his reign many poets, calligraphers, and painters appeared. The Tang Poem has its own style and it has been highly appreciated and preserved by the Chinese.

In 646, Li Shimin fell ill and died in 649. It is suspected that he was killed by taking the wrong remedy.

Left: Li Shimin (Emperor Tang Zhenguan) has been hailed as a model emperor, in particular for his sensible approach to trading with foreigners. Here, he is depicted meeting with Songsän Gampo, in a painting on a scroll by Yan Liben. (*The Palace Museum*)

Queen Wu Zetian
(624–705)
Name: Wu Mei

Smitten by a member of his concubine, Emperor Tang Gaozong gave her the name Wu Mei and made her his empress. Unlike most of females of that time, Wu Mei could read and write and was a poet herself. On becoming the empress, she was involved in state affairs and learned how to manipulate policies. When Tang Gaozong died her sons became emperors one after another. Being dissatisfied with their performances, she inaugurated herself as Queen Zetian and changed the Dynasty to Zhou.

Although she implemented many liberal policies, she ruled with an iron fist and was not well liked.

On her death she was buried next to her husband, Tang Gaozong. Because most of officials who were employed by her were remnants from the Tang court, when it came to build her gravestone they were reluctant to archive this part of history, which was dominated by her. In the end, no decisions were made and the stone was left empty. This was the first Wordless Stone in China's history.

Below and right: Former concubine Wu Mei knew how to manipulate court matters, first with her husband, Emperor Tang Gaozong, and then with her sons as they became emperors.

Emperor Tang Ming

(685–762)
Name: Li Longji
Memorial name: Tang Xuanzong

The Chinese say it is easier to set up a business than to sustain it. And the same can be said for prolonging the imperial dynasties. The Tang Dynasty had a few strong leaders at the beginning. Li Longji was one of them. At the beginning of his era, the Tang had reached its pinnacle and started showing signs of declining. And Li Longji's negligence in the administration during the latter part of his reign only accelerated the end of the Tang Dynasty.

According to the Tang national census, the population had reached 53 million. The economy was still growing and trade continued with foreign countries via the Silk Road and the sea. Buddhism, Daoism, and many more religious beliefs were popular. The state book conservation program reached 53,915 volumes as well as producing some key poets and musicians.

However, Li Longji made Yang Yuhuan an empress. He neglected his responsibilities and focused only on spending time with her. Some state officials, including Yang Yuhuan's brother, took over the court authority without him noticing. After the "Anshi Coup," Li Longji was forced to flee and his son inherited the throne in 755. Yang Yuhuan was executed for disrupting the administration. Ever after, Li Longji was in a depressed state and died in 762.

Above: "Everything in the garden was rosy…" until Li Longji's court became exasperated at his neglect of his administrative duties in favor of spending time with his empress Yang Yuhuan.

NORTHERN SONG DYNASTY
(960-1127)

Emperor Taizu
(927–976)
Name: Zhao Kuangyin
Memorial name: Song Taizu

In 960, Zhao Kuangyin seized control of the armies from the Zhou Dynasty. He lied when he reported that the country was under attack in the North, and in fact initiated a coup to overthrow the Zhou regime. The Song Dynasty began.

Learning from previous experience of handing power over to individual generals and officials in order to control the administration, as soon as he established the Song sovereignty he held a banquet with the generals serving the Zhou Dynasty, and hinted to them that they could give up their power for good benefits and obey the Song administration. Many followed. From then on, his policies were oriented around developing the economy, education, and science, and avoiding military movements. In October, 976, Zhao Kuangyin was drinking one night with his brother Zhao Guangyi and died suddenly the next morning.

Above: Chen Qiao Tavern, where Zhao Kuangyin's coup occurred.

Emperor Song Renzong

(1010–1063)
Name: Zhao Zhen
Memorial name: Song Renzong

Zhao Zhen was known as a very disciplined emperor. On one occasion he read until late in the night and wanted a lamb stew to warm up. But he didn't want to disturb the chef and waited until the next morning. The empress pressed upon him to do what he wanted in the future. He explained that if the chefs knew he would like to eat late at night, they would be on alert every day to cook for him at that time, which would add extra work for the staff, as well as adding expenses for the palace.

His modest personality and liberal policy attracted many talented people to work for him, Judge Bao Zheng, for example. During his reign, to curb corruption, the law was modified so that if a monarch committed a crime he would be treated in the same way that civilians were. His administration also launched the first paper currency, called "Guan Jiao Zi" (Official Trading Note).

Below: Judge Bao Zheng, who acted as an adviser to Emperor Song Renzong.

Emperor Song Yingzong

(1052–1067)
Name: Zhao Shu
Memorial name: Song Yingzong

Zhao Shu fell ill not long after he was enthroned. The administration was taken care of by Dowager Cao. During his short four-year-reign, he provided full support to scholars who wanted to chronicle Chinese history, and the first edition of one of the most important archives was published— *Zi Zhi Tong Jian* (Chronicles of the Dynasties).

Right: An actor portraying Emperor Song Yingzong, whose name means "Outstandingly Talented Ancestor."

Emperor Song Shenzong

(1048–1085)
Name: Zhao Xu
Memorial name: Tang Xuanzong

Unlike his ancestors, Zhao Xu became interested in martial arts at a very young age. He believed in the theory that a prosperous country must have a strong army. The adviser Wang Anshi carried out the reform to support this theory. However, the reform was more biased to the rich landlords than to civilians, and layered bureaucracy also affected the growth of the economy.

Below: Emperor Song Shenzong (seen here in a modern reenactment) recruited adviser Wang Anshi to implement famous reforms that would benefit peasantry and the unemployed.

Emperor Song Zhezong

(1076–1100)
Name: Zhao Xi
Memorial name: Song Zhezong

Zhao Xi was put on the emperor's seat at age ten, but the administration was mainly controlled by Dowager Gao. She appointed Sima Guang as the prime minister and banned all the previous policies made by adviser Wang Anshi. Zhao Xi didn't like the pressure and as soon as Dowager Gao died he demoted Sima Guang, re-employed Wang Anshi, and reverted to the previous policies. Wang Anshi was seen as a good politician and economist. Some of his economic policies were believed to lead to the earliest form of national banks. However, the implementation was poorly executed and the reform failed during Zhao Xi's reign.

Left: Artistic depiction of the powerless Emperor Song Zhezong (also shown above), who was guided and controlled by the regent Empress Dowager Gao.

Emperor Song Huizong

(1082–1135)
Name: Zhao Ji
Memorial name: Song Huizong

Zhao Ji was best known for his accomplishments in art. He created a state gallery, inviting painters and writers. He then collected many of their artworks. "Along the River During the Qingming Festival" is a superb scroll some 1,735 feet long. It depicts the prosperous life-style in Kaifeng during the Qingming Festival. Zhao Ji commented on this scroll and added it to his collection. This gigantic painting is as important in Chinese art history as the Mona Lisa is in the West. It is now kept at the Palace Museum in Beijing.

In 1126, under attack by the Jin Dynasty in the north, Zhao Ji abdicated the throne in favor of his son, Zhao Huan, Song Qinzong.

Right: A portrayal of Emperor Song Huizong, noted for his artistic accomplishments and collection.

Emperor Song Qinzong

(1100–1156)
Name: Zhao Huan
Memorial name: Song Qinzong

Zhao Huan was obliged to inherit the crown when the Jins launched a military force to Song's northern borders and captured his brother Zhao Ji. He lacked experience and kept losing at the battlefront. In 1126, the Jin army approached Bianjing (modern-day Kaifeng). Before the troops were even close to the capital, Zhao Huan was prepared to surrender and eventually was captured and held as a hostage.

The Jin army packed up many of his and his brother's collections and shipped them to the north. In 1127, they conquered Bianjing and ended the Song Dynasty.

Below: A modern-day depiction of Zhao Huan (left) and attendant.

Right: A model showing the street layout of the city of Kaifeng around the time of Emperor Song Qinzong's reign.

SOUTHERN SONG DYNASTY
(1127–1279)

Emperor Song Gaozong

(1107–1187)
Name: Zhao Gou
Memorial name: Song Gaozong

Under attack by the Jin, Zhao Gou escaped to the south and enthroned himself as an emperor in Nanjing, calling it Song Dynasty. Historians call it Southern Song Dynasty. Enjoying his supremacy, he was assisted by Qin Hui in murdering General Yue and his family so that the Jin would continue to keep his father as a hostage. At the same time, he continued to sign various treaties, giving up lands and monies in return for peace. He resigned in 1162.

Right: General Yue of the Song Dynasty enjoying horseback fighting trials shortly before he was executed by Zhaogao.

WESTERN XIA DYNASTY
(1038–1227)

Emperor Xia Jingdi
(1003–1048)
Name: Li Yuanhao
Memorial name: Xia Jingdi

Li Yuanhao was originally from Tangut, the son of the Tangut ruler, Li Deming. In 1038 he declared independence from the Song Dynasty. Repeatedly through diplomatic approaches, he asked the Song Dynasty to acknowledge Western Xia as an independent state but the Song administration would not agree and instead sent troops to provoke wars.

The three major battles between the Song and Western Xia— Sanchuankou, Haoshuichua, and Dingchuan—all ended with the Song losing. However, the Song Dynasty ruled a much stronger country and could afford the war expenses. Despite winning, Li Yuanhao was all but bankrupt. Once again he sent the diplomat Li Wengui to sue for reconciliation, resulting in the signing of the Dongjing (modern-day Kaifeng) Treaty. The war finally ended.

In 1048, Li Yuanhao attempted to abandon the title of crown prince for his son, Ning Lingge. In retaliation, Ning Lingge tried to murder his father, but failed. Li Yuanhao's nose was slit and he died from the injury shortly after.

YUAN DYNASTY
(1271–1368)

Genghis Khan

(1162-1227)
Name: Temüjin (Tiemu Zhen in Chinese)
Memorial name: Yuan Taizu

In the Mongol language, "Khan" means "Ruler." Temüjin founded his empire through battles and military force. He was a tough warrior and in over sixty battles that he led his forces through, there was only one war in which he found

himself in a losing state—"the 13 Wing Battle." But in the end, his opponent's tribe rebelled and joined with Genghis Khan anyway. He established a Mongol republic by uniting all nomadic tribes, and was given Yuan Taizu's name to commemorate his success in building the foundation of the Yuan Dynasty. He announced the "Laws of Genghis Khan," said to be the most complete law in the world at that time.

Genghis Khan, however, never stopped there. He kept redrawing Mongolia's maps and borders by invading his neighbors. In 1227 he died after winning the battle against Tangut.

Far left: A battler all his life, Genghis Khan was Mongol founder and ruler, and was named (posthumously) Khagan (emperor).

Left: Genghis Khan, a warrior dressed for battle,

Right: A bust of Genghis Khan, who established a Mongol republic by force of arms.

Great Khan

(1186–1241)
Name: Ögedei Khan
Memorial name: Yuan Taizong

Ögedei Khan was the third son of Genghis Khan. He inherited not only the title but also the tasks of his father. During his reign, he continued the military movement towards the West, to Europe as well as South China. However, a series of his policies, such as establishing tax offices and setting up the Central Administration Office, revealed signs that he was hoping to separate military power from government administration. He deeply believed in Confucianism, and built The Confucius Temple, held national Confucius exams, and eliminated taxes for Confucian scholars.

In 1234 he conquered Jin and erased another opponent of Mongolia before establishing the Yuan Dynasty. While trying to conquer Western Europe in 1241, Ögedei Khan suddenly died. His descendants never completed this mission. It is said this marked the end of the Mongol military movement towards the West.

Above: Ogedai Khan (Great Khan), who continued the expansion of the empire that his father Genghis Khan had begun.

Kublai Khan

(1215–1294)
Name: Borjigin Kublai
Memorial name: Yuan Shizu

Kublai Khan was in fact the first emperor of the Yuan Dynasty but he was the last Khan of the Mongol republic established by Genghis Khan. He didn't lose Mongolia, instead he finally ended the Song Dynasty and extended the Mongolian map to the entirety of China, as well as keeping the areas his family had already conquered.

Understanding that Chinese culture is the soul of Asia, in order to better rule China and Asia he moved the capital to Yanjing (modern-day, Beijing) and changed the name of his empire to Yuan. In general he adopted the Chinese system for administration, implemented Chinese law, and divided the country into provinces for easier management. He made massive investments to build roads across the Yuan Dynasty. Trees were planted with even gaps along these roads; taverns for travelers and horses to rest were provided. These roads were also used as the network for nationwide services.

During his reign, paper currency was officially passed as the means for trading. For the system to take off, the government announced a series of product prices as the standards for trading.

Many of the stories about Kublai Khan were learned through the Italian traveler Marco Polo. Yanjing, the capital of the Yuan Dynasty, was the largest city in the world, attracting visits by people from all over the globe. It took four years for the Italian merchant to travel to China. After seventeen years in China, often spent close to Kublai Khan, he returned to Italy and published *The Travels of Marco Polo*. The book described China in great detail and intrigued the Europeans, especially those in Western Europe, who were fascinated with its rich Oriental culture.

In the latter part of his life, Kublai Khan may have fallen into a state of depression when he lost his crown prince. He died of severe gout.

Above: Grandson of Genghis Khan, Kublai Khan established the Yuan Dynasty, and became emperor of all China.

Emperor Yuan Chengzong

(1265–1307)
Name: Borjigin Temür
Memorial name: Yuan Chengzong

Borjigin Temür's policy was more focused on domestic issues rather than extending the territories of the Yuang Dynasty. His administrations conducted a full research on local issues first, then were targeted on problematic regions, some of which received immediate tax deduction. At the same time, he stressed the importance of improving agricultural productivity. To further improve the stability in the south, he halted the invasion of Vietnam. Instead, he tried various diplomatic approaches, such as offering finances, arranging connections via marriages, or providing bureaucratic titles to remote regions. If any of his own officers were caught for corruption, Borjigin Temür brought them to justice.

Apparently, war was no longer the only solution during his reign. When he was provoked to go to war with Japan in 1299, he instead sent a diplomat and expressed the idea of re-establishing the relationships through trade and cultural communications. Later in his reign,

he did send troops to repress the ethnic war and finally settled them with force.

Above: Borjigin Temür favored diplomacy instead of combat.

Emperor Yuan Renzong

(1311–1320)
Name: Borjigin Ayurparibhadra
Memorial name: Yuan Renzong

Ayurparibhadra studied Confucianism from when he was a child. During his reign, he pushed for reforms to adopt the Chinese system. He ordered many Chinese classic books, such as *Chronicles of the Dynasties* (Zi Zhi Tong Jian), to be translated into Mongolian so that various ethnic groups could study the Chinese culture. Even though the Mongolians had not conquered the Song Dynasty in the south, he already asked the Yuan Dynasty to set up a parallel national exam system to recruit civil servants in the Chinese way.

His reign lasted for only nine years. During this time, he pushed Mongolia (Yuan Dynasty) one step forward towards a Chinese-Mongolian integrated country.

Above: Commercial ties with European countries increased during the reign of Emperor Yuan Renzong.

Emperor Yuan Wenzong

(1304–1332)
Name: Borjigin Toq-Temür
Memorial name: Yuan Wenzong

Borjigin Toq-Temür was a fearless nomadic character, but also a serious reader and painter as well as an accomplished poet. During his reign, he focused on literary development of the Yuan Dynasty. For instance, he gathered people together to write and edit archives such as those of some of the previous Chinese dynasties. Besides historical research, he promoted the study of other subjects such as woodwork, bridgework, architecture, gem craft, gold craft, and many more. The resulting multi-volume work—*Jing Shi Da Dian* (World References)—is greatly appreciated by historians studying the relationships between Yuan and the European countries, and how they exchanged knowledge and experiences in many skills such as agriculture, trades, and sailing.

Above: Borjigin Toq-Temür became the emperor of China as well as ruling as emperor of the Yuan Dynasty, the empire of the Great Khan.

Emperor Yuan Nizong

(1326–1332)
Name: Borjigin Irinchibal
Memorial name: Yuan Nizong

Tugh Temür Toghun, in order to avoid the suspicion that he killed his brother, Kuśala, insisted on not having Toghan-Temür, the eldest son of Kuśala, inherit the crown. The excuse given was that Toghan-Temür was away in Yunnan. Instead, Irinchibal, the youngest son, was chosen as a "baby emperor" at age seven. Irinchibal, however, died after just forty-three days. Toghun Temür was called back to the throne.

By the 14th Century, the Yuan administration had already lost control over regional governments. Rebellions were taking place all over the country. In 1368, Zhu Yuanzhang created the Ming sovereign, first in the south, and then led the army towards the north. As the troops approached Dadu (modern-day Beijing), the capital of the Yuan Dynasty, Toghan Temür escaped. Twice he resisted the Ming forces in Shangdu, north of Dadu, but he failed. A year later, he set up the Northern Yuan Dynasty in Inner Mongolia.

Above: Irinchibal was chosen as emperor at age seven, but he died a few weeks later.

MING DYNASTY
(1368–1644)

Emperor Ming Hongwu

(1328–1398)
Name: Zhu Yuanzhang
Memorial name: Ming Taizu

One of the only two emperors who arose from farmers' rebellions in Chinese history (the other being Liu Bang), Zhu Yuanzhang was inaugurated in Nanjing in 1368. In contrast to Liu Bang, he was extremely sensitive about his peasant background. His cold-blooded persecution of the intellectual officials proved his ignorance. During his reign, official writing was carefully observed for any slight hint of opposition against authority. Minor mistakes or implications of disagreement towards him could cause instant execution to the offending officer.

Zhu Yuanzhang implemented a series of agricultural policies in 1370 to encourage people to explore and grow crops in barren lands in the north. Later, the policies became more forceful. Many peasants were moved to the deserted areas but provided with state investments of agricultural tools and materials. Farmers were also allowed to keep their lands after cultivating them. Soon after, more effort was made by the emperor to improve the water system, mainly for farming needs. At the end of his reign, the number of newly cultivated lands reached 40,987 pieces with the support of 4,162 water-engine canals. Enhanced productivity of food and vegetation helped ease the pressure of lack of food caused by the increased population, and thus the economy boomed.

Hongwu was aggrieved at the corruption and betrayal, and instituted extremely harsh laws against corruptive behavior throughout the government from local regions to the central court. This was contrary to the tradition of the barbarians' adaptation of the Chinese system. Hongwu inherited many of the execution methods from the Mongol government, Yuan Dynasty. He died in 1398, having been the longest living emperor in the Ming Dynasty.

Emperor Ming Wendi

(1377–?)
Name: Zhu Yunwen
Memorial name: Ming Huizong

Emperor Ming Yongle

(1360–1424)
Name: Zhu Di
Memorial name: Ming Taizong, Ming Chengzu

A grandson of Hongwu, Wendi was described as a mild-tempered Confucian idealist. He attempted to amend the Ming laws and principles to ban the harsh punishments. Within four years of his reign, criminal offences decreased to only thirty percent of the levels they had been under the previous government. This tolerance immediately won him respect among officials and intellectuals.

Among many of his open-minded reforms was the invalidation of the dukeships. Most of the duke titles were held by the emperor's uncles. However, Wendi's sympathies failed to eliminate the power of the most aggressive uncle, Zhu Di, the Duke of Yan, who governed Beijing.

One night in June 1399, Zhu Di conquered Nanjing by force. Wendi disappeared from the court, which led to one of the most mysterious and unsolved investigations in Chinese history. Having high respect for Emperor Wendi, the majority of his officers refused to serve his uncle Zhu Di, and they either escaped or were executed.

Left: Emperor Hongwu, founder and first emperor of the Ming Dynasty, led an army that during a period of plagues, famine, and peasant revolts, ended the Yuan Dynasty and drove the Mongols to the Mongolian steppes.

Right: Third emperor of the Ming Dynasty, Zhu Di ordered the renovation of the Grand Canal, a massive undertaking that took thirteen years to complete, aiding the commercial communication between north and south China.

Originally Duke of Yan (modern-day Beijing), Zhu Di crowned himself as the third emperor of the Ming Dynasty after stealing the reign from his nephew. In 1403, he was inaugurated as the Emperor Yongle in Nanjing, still the

capital of the Ming Dynasty. Soon after, he felt he was more accustomed to living in Beijing and the northern culture. In 1422, Ming was recapitalized in Beijing and Zhu Di became the first Han Chinese emperor in this northern city.

To stabilize the economy of Beijing and ensure the supplies to the construction of the Forbidden City, his palace, Zhu Di ordered the renovation of the Grand Canal. It took nine years to clear this ancient channel between the south and the north and it was up to thirteen years before transportation on the canal was running smoothly. Construction of the Forbidden City lasted fourteen years. The canal continued to play an important role in the connection between north and south China, in many respects.

Almost an economist himself, Zhu Di believed that the sufficiency of materials to each family and prosperous trade were the fundamentals of peace. Not only did he encourage domestic trading, but supported the voyages of explorer Zhenghe, who sailed overseas seven times, trading with over thirty countries. Through Zhenghe's visits, diplomats from many countries were invited to China for further cultural exchanges.

At the same time, Zhu Di did not neglect archiving the history of the Ming and previous dynasties. He ordered state libraries to be set up, calling for antique books to be sent to the central libraries to build state collections. Over three thousand people were devoted to rebinding more than eight thousand collectible volumes, including a vast collection of Chinese literature, history, and philosophy covering many subjects. By 1408, some 11,095 volumes had been rebound and were named as one collection, *Yongle Great Encyclopedia*.

A wise and effective military commander throughout his life, Yongle died at age sixty-four during a military campaign to the Gobi Desert, and was buried in Chang Ling, the Ming Tomb Group in Northwest Beijing.

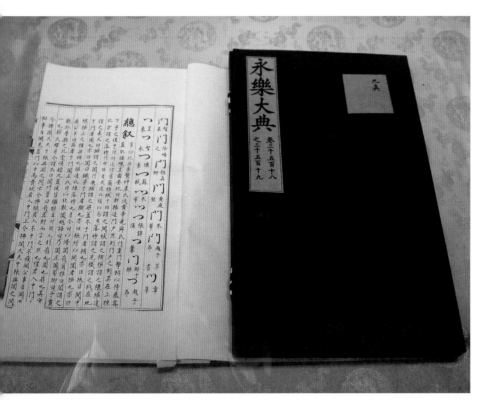

Left: Completed under Emperor Ming Yongle in 1408, the *Yongle Great Encyclopedia* contained 11,095 volumes.

Emperor Ming Hongxi

(1378–1425)
Name: Zhu Gaozhi
Memorial name: Ming Renzong

Zhu Gaoxi, a grandson of Taizu, was one of the most popular heirs, for his reserved manner and talent. Acting as the key adviser to Chengzu Zhu Di, his policies were already widely implemented before his crowning as emperor.

Knowing the rigorous punishments legitimized by Zhu Di, Zhu Gaozhi immediately released some innocent prisoners from the previous reign. Many of them were kin families or officers who served at court. Being aware that the big palace in Beijing was costly to maintain, to reduce the expense to the government he decided to move his residence back to Nanjing. He also stopped the collection of luxurious goods for the imperial family and halted the regular overseas travel by sea. Traditionally, more southern intellectuals used to serve in court due to their high scores from exams; so to balance the power at court between the south and north he initiated the South-Sixty-North-Forty rule so that the northern people were encouraged to work harder and thus join the court.

Zhu Gaozhi died of a heart attack after only ten months in government, but was highly regarded for his refinement of various policies.

Above: As soon as he became emperor, Zhu Gaozhi cancelled what he saw as wasteful projects, such as maritime expeditions, in favor of many reforms that had a good and lasting effect on the wellbeing of his subjects.

Emperor Ming Xuande

(1398–1435)
Name: Zhu Zhanji
Memorial name: Ming Xuanzong

In order to relieve the economic burden on his people, Zhu Zhanji instituted a policy of reducing troops at borders and maintaining peace with neighboring countries. This allowed him to reduce the levy of agricultural produce, and later provide governmental relief in the event of natural disasters. He died at age thirty-eight of an unknown disease. A calligrapher and painter, the emperor left behind many written and painted masterpieces, such as "Verse of Snow" and "Monkey Play." His reign was often referred to as the Ming Golden Age.

Below: Life was more peaceful under Emperor Ming Xuande, as indicated by this scroll painting of aristocrats enjoying a leisurely day's hunting (the figure on the white horse at top left is believed to be the emperor). *(The Palace Museum)*

Emperor Ming Zhengtong or Tian Shun

(1427–1464)
Name: Zhu Qizhen
Memorial name: Ming Yingzong

Legend has it that Zhu Qizhen was the son of a palace servant, but stolen at birth by the Empress Sun who couldn't bear children. As the heir apparent, he was crowned at age nine, but was imprisoned by the Mongols at age twenty-two after being defeated in the Battle of Tumu Fortress. It was a war that could have been avoided, yet the young and self-assured emperor drafted 500,000 troops to head to the north, only to be completely shattered.

The Mongols returned Zhu Qizhen to the Ming court a year later. He was, however, carefully watched by Emperor Jingtai, who was enthroned during Zhu Qiyu's absence. This house arrest lasted for seven years until Emperor Jingtai fell ill. An opportunity presented itself and Zhu Qizhen overthrew his uncle to recapture the throne. The second era of Zhu Qizhen's reign was named as Tian Shun. A much more mature leader this time, he died only three years later.

Below: An observatory in Beijing believed to have been built in the period 1435 to 1464 during which Zhu Qizhen reigned twice as emperor.

Emperor Ming Jingtai
(1428–1457)
Name: Zhu Qiyu
Memorial name: Ming Daizong

When Zhu Qizhen was captured by the Mongols after the Battle of Tumu Fortress, the heir-apparent Zhu Jianju was only two years old. Zhu Qiyu followed the empress's lead and took over the responsibility to become the emperor, and named his era Jingtai. Once he took over the throne, however, Zhu Qiyu tried every means to avoid having anything to do with Zhu Qizhen. A year later, when Zhu Qizhen was sent back by the Mongols, Emperor Jingtai had him placed under house arrest and carefully had his every movement watched in an isolated section of the Forbidden City.

His own heir-apparent's sudden death, which was thought to be murder, struck a devastating blow to Zhu Qiyu, such that he fell ill. Zhu Qizhen took advantage of this opportunity and became the emperor again.

The next year, until his last breath, Zhu Qiyu could not fight back, and did not even consider naming another heir. Zhu Qizhen didn't honor him with an emperor's memorial nor was he given a tomb at

the Ming imperial shrine. Instead, he was buried in the west side of Beijing according to his dukeship. Later, he was awarded with a memorial name, as with all other emperors.

Above: Zhu Qiyu was appointed emperor (Jingtai) while his older brother Zhu Qizhen was held prisoner by the Mongols. Detained for a year, Zhu Qizhen was released but placed under house arrest by Jingtai, who granted him the meaningless title "grand-emperor."

Emperor Ming Chenghua

(1447–1487)
Name: Zhu Jianshen
Memorial name: Ming Xianzong

The original name of Emperor Ming Chenghua was Zhu Jianjun. When his father was re-inaugurated, he received a new name, Zhu Jianshen, and was promoted as heir-apparent for the second time. He was said to be not as competitive as his father. After becoming the emperor himself, he was unwilling to take revenge for the restraint of himself and his father by Zhu Qiyu. Even his chancellors recommended that he execute the remaining princes, chancellor and empresses of the Jingtai era, but he turned down the request by signing the document as, "I am not bothered by the past incidence."

Policies of tolerance were implemented throughout the court and the rest of the nation. China took advantage of a few years' peace during his reign, being involved in very few external conflicts and domestic rebellions.

Among many other artistic emperors of the Ming Dynasty, Zhu Jianshen was renowned for his excellent portrait painting and left behind a few masterpieces of portraits of people who lived during his reign.

Below: Zhu Jianshen enjoying watching a game of football (soccer) during a peaceful time in China's evlution. He was said to be a calm individual, not interested in taking revenge for he and his father having been restrained by previous administrations. *(The Palace Museum)*

Right: While his father was under house arrest, Zhu Jianshen lived under the shadow of his uncle Zhu Qiyu (Emperor Ming Jingtai), becoming emperor when the latter died in 1457.

Emperor Ming Hongzhi

(1470–1505)
Name: Zhu Youtang
Memorial name: Ming Xiaozong

The archives written by Qing Dynasty historians about the Ming are usually very critical of the Ming leaders. Zhu Youtang was an exception. Many stories record examples of how tolerant and understanding he was to his officials.

Until the Ming Dynasty, the ritual rules in court to maintain the emperors' supremacy were strict to the extreme. Any careless behavior from the officials or servants could be condemned as disrespectful to the emperors, therefore subject to punishment. Zhu Youtang was the most relaxed about it. Moreover, when he found out that some state officials had to travel home in the dark after visiting court, he arranged the palace guards to hold torches and accompany them home, no matter what their ranks or hierarchy. While some Ming emperors like Zhu Di would send the state marines to search for treasures around the world, Zhu Youtang set an example of living a prudent life-style. He once told a Korean diplomat, "... I am not into gems and treasures; snowy or windy, our administration is in operation; at our courteous banquets, we have cancelled music and performances to keep them simple..."

Unlike most of the Chinese emperors in history, Zhu Youtang married only one empress, raising two sons. One of them succeeded as Emperor Ming Zhengde.

Below: Typically courteous of him, Emperor Ming Hongzhi has attendants offer food to his advisers as they await an audience. *(The Palace Museum)*

Right: Zhu Youtang became a wise and tolerant emperor (Ming Hongzhi) who strove for a peaceful life for his people.

Emperor Ming Zhengde

(1491–1521)
Name: Zhu Houzhao
Memorial name: Ming Wuzong

As the tenth emperor of the long-lasting Ming Dynasty, Zhu Houzhao seemed to have lost his focus on state affairs. During his reign of sixteen years, he took his responsibility of government lightly but found various ways of entertaining himself.

He gave up the palace, the Forbidden City, and moved into a house where he raised leopards and tigers as a hobby, along with his harems of beautiful female entertainers. Once in a while, administrative work was carried out at this residence, which he kept expanding to as many as two hundred rooms. After taking interest in various religions from ethnic groups such as Islamic and Lamaist, he banned raising pigs and eating pork throughout China. When the main hall in the Forbidden City caught fire, he cheered as if it was a grand firework display.

Traveling was another of his extravagances. Besides wandering around Beijing, he also abandoned his routine imperial life and visited South China. During one of the return trips from the south, he imitated a fisherman casting a net and fell into the water, which caused him to become ill. Never recovering from the illness nor ceasing his activities, he exhausted himself to death eight months later.

Above: Despite early expectations that he would become a great ruler, Zhu Houzhao neglected his duties, permitting the rise of powerful eunuchs that would eventually dominate and ruin the Ming Dynasty.

Emperor Ming Jiajing

(1507–1567)
Name: Zhu Houcong
Memorial name: Ming Shizong

Fun-loving emperor Ming Zhengde didn't leave an heir, and Zhu Houcong was chosen for the crown by the imperial circle for his highly respected father, Zhu Youyuan. According to historians, after becoming an emperor, Zhu Houcong was comparable in many aspects to previous emperors, if not exceeding them, in his cruelty, control, ridicule, and arrogance.

Zhu Houcong grew up in South China where Daoism was a popular belief. One of the focuses of Daoism is longevity. The emperor tried every means within his capability to test various herbs to find the one medicine that could maintain his long life. In his reign, believers of Daoism were appreciated and anyone questioning this religion and the superstitious practicing of it could lead to them being publicly beaten to death. In 1542, many maids in the palace became sick after tasting the emperor's new nutritious longevity supplement, which caused a rare group assassination attempt against him. When the assassination attempt failed, everyone involved in the event

was executed. The emperor then moved his residence to the Wanshou Traveling Palace outside the Forbidden City in West Beijing, focusing with renewed vigor on researching herbal supplements.

Twenty years later, before his last breath, Zhu Hongcong was transported back to the Forbidden City. He died at age sixty, one of the longest living emperors of the Ming Dynasty. It was suspected that his practice of self-medicating with longevity supplements was the cause of his death.

Left: Zhu Houcong reigned as emperor for forty-five years during a period of apparent stability, but neglect of his official duties led the Ming Dynasty into gradual decline.

Right: Statue of a warrior at the Ming Tomb, where Emperor Ming Jiajing would have been buried. Cruel and arrogant, he clearly feared death, and constantly searched for medicines to extend his life. However, he died in 1567, probably from ingestion of mercury contained in his elixirs.

Emperor Ming Longqing

(1537–1572)
Name: Zhu Zaihou
Memorial name: Ming Muzong

A cautious and reserved emperor , Zhu Zaihou was highly regarded by his courtiers for his understated personality and management skills, and for trusting in his people.

During his reign, the country was experiencing a boosted economy, displaying a prosperous China once again. The emperor, however, was very careful with the state's costs,

Right: The prudent Emperor Ming Longqing inherited a country riven by mismanagement and corruption and could not halt the decline before he died at age thirty-five.

Below: Typical walled garden approach to a Ming Dynasty tomb.

Above: Entrance gate to the tomb of Emperor Ming Longqing.

including expenses for himself.

Historians appraised the emperor as one of the few upstanding, humble, and prudent emperors in Chinese history. Before his death after suffering a stroke, he regretted that he had over-indulged himself.

There were many sharp-minded counselors emerging to support the emperor in managing state affairs. Yet, due to the unprejudiced personality of the emperor himself, power-seeking conflicts quietly snowballed, resulting in clashes within the imperial families later.

Emperor Ming Wanli

(1563–1620)
Name: Zhu Yijun
Memorial name: Ming Shenzong

Zhu Yijun was crowned at ten years of age, and it was the statesman Zhang Juzheng who supported him in order to sustain the state affairs. For ten years, society progressed in a stable environment until Zhang Juzheng died. At the age of twenty, Zhu Yijun began to administer the country of his own accord.

A very hard-working emperor, Zhu Yijun was also a calligrapher. His stories of obeying and respecting his teacher and Zhang Juzheng were widely spread legends in court, winning him esteem from courtiers from his era as well as from later descendants.

During the war to assist Korea against the Japanese invasion in 1592, his strategies helped the Korean forces to defend their homeland, and in addition the preparation and exercising for war strengthened the Ming army and marine forces as well

Right: Emperor Ming Wanli took control of the administration at age twenty, but neglected his duties during the last two decades of his reign, causing a major decline in the Ming Dynasty's progress.

as the northern border in the east. However, when the Japanese, led by Toyotomi Hideyoshi, invaded for the second time in two years, the Ming army suffered great casualties and the defense was costly. Because of Zhu Yijun's lack of attention to the administration, the last twenty years of his reign sent the Ming Dynasty back to the dawn ages. In the 47th year of the Wanli reign, 1619, the Ming troops of 200,000 men were defeated by the Jurchen tribes in northeast China, led by military genius Nurhachi.

Zhu Yijun died in 1620 and was buried in Dingling, one of the largest Ming tombs. Later study of his tomb and mummified body suggested that he could have been a habitual user of opium.

Above: Two official headdresses made for Zhu Yijun (Emperor Ming Wanli).

Right: A gem-encrusted official headdress made for a Ming Dynasty empress. (The *Palace Museum*)

Emperor Ming Taichang

(1582–1620)
Name: Zhu Changluo
Memorial name: Ming Guangzong

Zhu Changluo was a thirty-day emperor, whose death became one of the most mysterious, unsolved stories of the Ming Dynasty. During the first fifteen days of his sovereignty, Zhu Changluo ordered a series of reforms including rewarding the troops serving at the Ming borders, lifting the taxation to various mines, and releasing officers who had been detained for making suggestions to Emperor Wanli from the previous era.

Then the new emperor became unexpectedly ill and was offered a herbal laxative from the imperial pharmacy as a remedy. After excreting thirty to forty times, he was given two red herbal capsules by an officer. After taking the first capsule the emperor appeared to be recovering, but was found dead the next morning after taking the second dose. This incident became known as the famous "Red Capsule Case." However, the investigation was never concluded.

Zhu Changluo was buried in the unused tomb that Emperor Jingtai built for himself among the Ming tomb group.

Above: Zhu Youyuan, Emperor Wanli, father of Zhu Changluo. *(The Palace Museum)*

Right: Emperor Ming Taichang, who died in circumstances still a mystery today. *(The Palace Museum)*

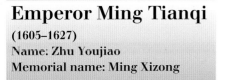

Emperor Ming Tianqi
(1605–1627)
Name: Zhu Youjiao
Memorial name: Ming Xizong

Zhu Youjiao was said to be a spoiled royal brat and was not prepared for the responsibility of emperorship that arrived at the sudden death of his father, Zhu Changluo. Besides the fact that the Ming Dynasty was continuing to decline in many ways, one of the major losses during his reign was Taiwan. In 1624, Dutch explorers conquered the entire island and the Ming Dynasty was incapable of regaining it.

The emperor was a talented carpenter. While chancellors such as Wei Zhongxian gradually stole the power and directed the government on his behalf, Zhu Youjiao was devoted to improving his carpentry skills. Much of the furniture, tools, and accessories for daily use in the palace were hand-crafted by the emperor himself. Zhu Youjiao was succeeded by his brother Chongzhen after his death in 1627.

Right: Zhu Youjiao was happy to indulge himself in his carpentry pastime, rather than running his country.

Emperor Ming Chongzhen

(1611–1644)
Name: Zhu Youjian
Memorial name: Ming Sizong

The last emperor of the Ming Dynasty, Zhu Youjian hanged himself in Jingshan Park, north of the Forbidden City. He had been enthroned at the age of eighteen, and proved to be hard working, prudent, and principled in dealing with the affairs of state. In 1628, Northern China and Henan Province were struck by drought and locust invasions. Li Zizheng led the farmers to rebel. The next year, a plague broke out across the country, and Beijing alone lost forty percent of the population due to disease and starvation. The country was about to go bankrupt. Then came the Manchurians, who attacked at the northeast border.

In 1644, Li Zicheng's rebellious group approached Beijing and the emperor was helpless. In his suicide note, he stated, "... I am guilty to have led the Ming Dynasty to this situation. I am too shameful to meet the ancestors. I resign and leave the robber (Li Zicheng) to treat my dead body as they wish. Just do not hurt any citizens."

Below: This is believed to be the tree from which Zhu Youjian hanged himself, taking the blame for disasters that befell the Ming Dynasty.

SHUN DYNASTY
(1644–1646)

Emperor Shun Tianqi
(1606–1646)
Name: Li Zicheng
Nickname: The Roaming King

Many people do not consider the Shun Dynasty as a dynasty at all since, compared with the Ming before and the Qing after, it was too minimal to be taken into account. However, when Li Zicheng took over Beijing, for the short period of time of his sovereignty he did proclaim himself as emperor of a new dynasty, Shun, which indeed became the transition dynasty until the Manchurians marched into Beijing.

Li Zicheng was interested in the martial arts from childhood. He once worked at a tavern and was fired for losing official paperwork. He joined his uncle to lead the farmers' rebellion against the Ming governorship, advocating the policy of even ownership of land and no tax for farmers around the country.

In 1644, he proclaimed himself emperor of the Shun Dynasty in Xi'an

and headed to the capital, threatening the Ming administration. A few days after battling around Beijing, he took residence in the Forbidden City, finishing the Ming Dynasty, until the Manchurian's invasion of Beijing the next year. Li Zicheng escaped and disappeared in Hubei Province.

Above: Li Zicheng, leader of the 1644 rebellion against the Ming Dynasty, and self-proclaimed emperor of the Shun Dynasty.

160

QING DYNASTY
(1644–1912)

Emperor Qing Tianming
(1559–1626)
Name: Aisin-Gioro Nurhachi
Memorial name: Qing Taizu

In 1584, Nurhachi united the Jurchens and established the first Manchu state—Great Jin. It was the foundation of Qing, one of the longest dynasties in Chinese history. Nurhachi was said to have grown up in a Han Chinese family. He was influence by Chinese culture and impressed by the Chinese language.

The Jurchens, after being conquered by the Mongols, borrowed the Mongolian language and didn't use their own. Nurhachi revised the Mongolian language by adding dots and points, transforming it into a new script used as Manchurian.

His ambition was to rule China. In 1625, he moved his capital to Shengjing (modern-day Shenyang) and started to attack the Ming border the following year. He was defeated by the Ming General Yuan Chonghuan and died eight months later.

Right: Emperor Qing Tianming, who established the first Manchu state, foundation of the Qing Dynasty.

Emperor Qing Tiancong, Qing Chongde
(1592–1645)
Name: Aisin-Gioro Huangtaiji
Memorial name: Qing Taizong

The eighth son of Nurachi, Huangtaiji became the second Khan of the Manchu Dynasty. Ten years into his reign, he changed his dynasty to Da Qing (The Great Qing). Although his father established the Aisin-Gioro empire, Huangtaiji was in fact the first emperor of the Qing Dynasty. To secure his position as the sole center of power, he took over all Eight Banners of troops by removing his three brothers from their leading military positions. At the same time, it was evident that the Manchurians needed to expand the size of their army if they were to invade China, Korea, and other neighboring countries. More and more Mongolian clans were being merged into the Qing system. Huangtaiji organized the Mongolians into Mongol Eight Banners too. Along with many Chinese who were moving to Manchu states, there were three Chinese generals who led all their troops to join him. They became the Han Eight Banners. With the three forces of the Manchu, Mongol, and Chinese, the Qing troops were much stronger and ready to invade China.

In the meantime, the Dongbei (northeast) region became a multi-cultural kingdom with various languages and life-styles. Besides the local Manchurians, Mongolians, and Han Chinese, there were also more and more clans of Jurchens. To compromise the Manchurians' emphasis on military development and weakness in literary management, Huangtaiji adopted the Ming political system and employed some Han Chinese to reform the Qing's administration.

To conquer China, Huangtaiji had one more concern—

General Yuan Chonghuan serving at Ming Chongzhen's court, whose troops camped at the Shanhai Gate of the Great Wall northeast of Beijing. Huangtaiji allied the Mongolians, bypassing the blockade set up by Yuan Chonghuan, and invaded via a detour that took him towards Beijing straight from the north. Yuan Chonghuang pulled his troops back to Beijing North, and managed to push Huangtaiji back to Mongolia. Shortly after, however, Yuan Chonghuan was imprisoned and executed for having a disagreement with the Ming emperor.

With this sole remaining barrier lifted, Huantaiji attacked again in 1642, resulting in the Ming border troops surrendering. However, Huantaiji died in September, a few months before his army finally marched into Beijing. Because of his success in establishing the Great Qing Dynasty through years of wars, Huantaiji was named by historians as the "Emperor on a Horseback."

Left: Huangtaiji built an army composed of Manchu, Mongol, and Chinese forces capable of overwhelming Beijing. (*The Palace Museum*)

Above: A decorative suit of armor made for Emperor Qing Tiancong, for dress purposes rather than for combat. (*The Palace Museum*)

Right: The saddle and accouterments made for Huantaiji, the "Emperor on a Horseback." (*The Palace Museum*)

Emperor Qing Shunzhi
(1638–1661)
Name: Aisin-Gioro Fulin
Memorial name: Qing Shizu

Fulin was appointed emperor at the age of six when his father Huangtaiji died. It was his uncle Aisin-Gioro Dorgon who stayed next to him to support the sovereign. When he was fourteen, Dorgon died. The Shunzhi era was to be administered by Fulin independently.

In 1644, the Qing army overthrew Li Zicheng and finally took over Beijing. Fulin in fact was the first Qing emperor who settled in Beijing. After generations of expansion, the Qing administration was under pressure as a result of the heavy expenses of war. Meanwhile, the Qing Dynasty had a tip-over from a Manchurian state to a country, in which Chinese made up most of its population. Fulin immediately signed off a series of political changes to adapt to this challenge.

A campaign started to enforce the idea that the Qing Dynasty was a state of Manchurians as well as the Han Chinese. They were "One Family." Confucianism was appreciated, while the ideals of the new administration and the Han Chinese would be eligible for participating in court. Through four major state exams, over a thousand Chinese were recruited to work for the administration. In addition to various ways of carrying through a smooth acquisition, Fulin's army reached deeper south to repel the organized rebels from the Han Chinese, who were still fighting for overturning China as a sole Chinese state.

Fulin died as young as twenty-four. Without

Right: With the Qing pacification of the former Ming provinces almost complete, Fulin died at the young age of twenty-four in circumstances that hae not been fully explained. *(The Palace Museum)*

clarification from the Qing court, many suspicions were raised about his death. One explanation was that he died of deep depression due to the loss of his son and a beloved empress. Another rumor was that he was devoted to Buddhism and quietly left the administration to become a monk.

Throughout his administration as well as the following reign—Qing Kangxi—Fulin's mother, Dowager Xiaozhuang, was said to be the backbone of the Qing Dynasty. When her emperor husband and son both died, she looked after the extensive imperial family as well as the dynasty, which was going through a difficult transition period.

Her achievements were well revealed through her relationship with her grandson Xuanye. During her later life, Xuanye, said to be one of the most successful emperors in Chinese history, regarded her as a mentor, a parent, and the real authority until her death at the age of seventy-five. The Dowager left her final letter dedicating her later life to her grandson Xuanye, whose love and respect helped her go through the tough times for her and the Qing Dynasty.

Right: Dowager Xiaozhuang, Fulin's mother, regarded as the backbone of the Qing Dynasty during the turbulent mid-1600s. *(The Palace Museum)*

Emperor Qing Gangxi

(1654–1722)
Name: Aisin-Gioro Xuanye
Memorial Name: Qing Shengzu

Emperor Gangxi was crowned at eight years old and governed for sixty-one years from the age of nineteen. He had the longest reign in Chinese history and is largely considered as one of the greatest emperors of China. The combined periods of rule of Gangxi and Emperor Qianlong, who reigned after him, became named as "The Golden Age of Kang-Qian." Later, in naming Gangxi's tomb, people addressed him as the "Qing Great Ancestor."

After the first three emperors of the Qing dynasty, Gangxi's policies strengthened the Manchurian government of China. He highly admired Chinese language, culture, and literature. A very well-read emperor, he studied Han Chinese history, learned about water engineering, and promoted Chinese intellectuals in his dynasty.

One of his most important resolutions was to strengthen the borders of China during the Qing Dynasty. When the Manchurians took power, in order to settle the remote ethnic feuds around China, the Qing government established the Fan policy—the special administration regions. These regions enjoyed different taxation standards and were entitled to keep their private military forces. But up to Gangxi's era, some of these regions grew much more powerful. They gradually pushed their borders further inland.

The growth of these regions proved it was difficult to control a different system from the remote central

Right: Emperor Qing Gangxi practicing calligraphy in casual attire.
(The Palace Museum)

167

government. Their own taxation not only did not bring profit to Beijing but also caused local repression. Emperor Gangxi decisively eliminated this structure. Some of the Fan governors took advantage of the change of policy and provoked regional wars in order to declare independence. Gangxi led his troops to various regions to face these protests. It took over eight years to calm these areas and reconcile control of them.

Gangxi respected that Tibetans looked up to their religious leaders as policy makers. On the one hand, he approved of the Dalai Lama leading Tibet, but on the other hand he increased his military presence in the Tibetan Highlands. Furthermore, his policy encouraged trade and communication between the Tibetans and the mainland Chinese.

At home, Gangxi paid close attention to his sons'

development in order to choose the right successor. Instead of naming his heir-apparent, he motivated the princes to study and work hard in order to compete with each other. Later, he wrote down his decision and hid the note in a box in Qianqing Hall at the palace, for the heir to be announced on his deathbed.

However, the competition among his numerous princes caused furious conflicts. Even though his fourth son was publicly announced as the chosen emperor, rumor has it that the original intention was for the fourteenth son to inherit the administration. A suspicious addition of one stroke to a written character could have altered the fate of both princes and the Qing Dynasty.

Above: Emperor Qing Gangxi and his entourage during his travels in South China, depicted in a painting on a scroll. *(The Palace Museum)*

Right: A musket made in England for Aisin-Gioro Xuanye, probably as a commercial gift. *(The Palace Museum)*

Emperor Qing Yongzheng

(1678–1755)
Name: Aisin-Gioro Yinzhen
Memorial name: Qing Shizong

Chinese scholar Yang Qijiao once said, "Without Yongzheng's house-cleaning, the Qing Dynasty would have ended much earlier." This reveals a great deal about Yinzhen's reign—Qing Yongzheng.

Yinzhen was the fourth son of Xuanye. When he became the third emperor of Qing, he focused on streamlining the government both within the central office and outside. His targets ranged from his brothers and extended family to officials around him and even those located remotely from Beijing, the center of the state. He was very diligent, and involved himself deeply in order to bring corrupt officers to justice.

In 1729, a Military Intelligent Agency, "Junjichu," was established to support the anti-corruption campaign. The office was located inside the Forbidden City, and was organized by the most trusted chancellors and supervised by Yinzhen himself. The agency proved to be efficient. Originally intended for temporary tasks, it was later turned into a permanent division for

emperors to direct military forces. Yinzhen himself and other emperors throughout this organization grasped the Holy Grail to the central power in controlling the gigantic Qing political system. (However, as the power of the Military Intelligent Agency grew, it became more and more corrupted, and later the biggest barrier to improving the government.)

Yinzhen was enthroned at age forty-five after many years of observing his father, the greatest emperor and politician in Chinese history. His reforms enhanced what his father had achieved and his detailed policies stabilized the economy from the bottom up. The most important policy concerned the taxation on farmers. Instead of arbitrarily collecting taxes for more income for the dynasty, his campaign focused on increasing food productivity. In the old days, farmers were imposed both a "citizen's tax" as well as a "land tax," meaning that even if they did not own the land the farmers still had to pay taxes. During natural disasters, the double burden caused many farmers to go bankrupt and leave their homes. Yinzhen merged the two taxes into one to induce farmers to stay with their lands and increase productivity. Lands were taxed according to labor intensity. The policy, although not suiting well-off landlords, paid off for the Manchurian authority. By the end of Yinzhen's reign, the state reserve was in fact more than what his father had collected.

The popular saying "Kang Qian Prosperity" refers to Kangxi's era headed by his father and Qian Long's era by his son. In fact, their successes would not have benefited the Qing sovereignty for over two hundred years without Yinzhen's transition period.

Left: A formal portrait of Emperor Qing Yongzheng (Aisin-Gioro Yinzhen), who had a direct hand in the establishment of the Military Intelligent Agency, "Junjichu,"

Right: Emperor Qing Yongzheng and his entourage (bottom left) enjoy a relaxing stroll in sumptuous surroundings. (*The Palace Museum*)

Emperor Qing Qianlong

(1711–1799)
Name: Aisin-Gioro Hongli
Memorial name: Qing Gaozong

Hongli was a famous Chinese emperor who is often associated with the era of "Kang Qian Prosperity." He is often compared with his grandfather Aixin-Gioro Xuanye, as well as Li Shimin from the Tang Dynasty. These three emperors are said to have brought China to the peak during their times. Besides his hard-working virtue, like that of his father and grandfather, and his liberal economic policies, Hongli was a productive poet, devoted calligrapher, brave general, and possibly one of the greatest diplomats in history.

One of the first policies Hongli implemented was to continue the tax reduction to farmers. It was focused on developing lands. Up to his reign, the Qing Dynasty had settled and ruled peacefully for three generations. The population continued to grow, up to two hundred million. More people needed more supplies. He applied zero tax to deserted areas, encouraging farmers to cultivate infertile lands. More people were willing to migrate to

Left: Aisin-Gioro Hongli (Emperor Qing Qianlong) armed with arrows. (The Palace Museum)

Below: Hongli practicing calligraphy in Han Chinese attire. (The Palace Museum)

remote areas and the development boosted the economy across the country.

More than any other emperor in history, Hongli traveled six times into the south, to inspect with his own eyes the Han-Chinese-concentrated regions. Although his extravagant traveling was costly, the results of the trips were significant to the cultural connections between the south and north of the Qing Dynasty and China. The Summer Palace, for example, was inspired by the southern-style gardens after Hongli visited some of the private gardens in Suzhou and Hangzhou.

The editing of *Sikuquanshu* (Siku Encyclopaedia) was another of his literary achievements. During Hongli's reign, scholars who raised some doubts regarding *Yongle Great Encyclopaedia* received support from the emperor. The project turned into one of an enormous movement in collecting existing books. From beginning to end, it took almost twenty years and 3,300 editors collecting, sorting, checking, editing, and copying over five hundred subjects and tens of thousands of existing books. The finished encyclopaedia included 36,000 volumes of four sections of Classics, History, Philosophy, and Literature. Hongli, among many of his Manchurian family members, admired the Chinese

Left: Hongli (seated) watches children making figures in the snow. (*The Palace Museum*)

Left: A travel case used by Emperor Qing Qianlong. (The Palace Museum)

Below: Aisin-Gioro Hongli apparently copied this calligraphy from Wang Xizhi, "The Sage of Calligraphy." *(The Palace Museum)*

culture. His passion for Chinese calligraphy, art, and poetry was shown through his own art works. In the name of such a great historical collective work, however, over 150,000 copies of what were thought to be anti-Qing books were destroyed forever.

To maintain Qing's reign, Hongli was also a tough military leader. He successfully repressed the Uiger rebellion in Xinjiang region in the west of China, and settled troops into the Tibetan highlands. The diplomatic approach, however, was even more effective in ruling the borderline ethnics. He invited the religious leaders to Beijing, and built temples, mosques, and shrines to help them spread their religious beliefs to a larger audience. The ethnic regions were settled and China then became much more culturally integrated among Manchurians, Mongols, Chinese, Muslims, and Tibetans.

It was during his administration, the Qing, that China and the imperial system were at their peaks. The prosperity was one of the reasons that kept China closing into herself until the Europeans opened the door with opium, canons, and guns. It was after Hongli's time that decline came to be more and more apparent until the end of the imperial system.

Emperor Qing Jiaqing

(1760–1820)
Name: Aisin-Gioro Yongyan
Memorial name: Qing Renzong

Yongyan's ancestors had almost perfected the system. But he found that to sustain the family dynasty was not enough. Bureaucracies grew from the massive political system. The conflicts between the policy makers and civilians turned more serious, which ignited some regional rebellions. It took Yongyan eighteen years to put out the fires caused by the "Tianlijiao" rebellious group.

In the meantime, opium quietly landed in some Chinese ports, by the British traders via India, and quickly became popular. The ban from the emperor was brisk and detailed rules were made. Users, traders, and officials involved would all be punished.

Yongyan was a deep believer in Confucianism. He granted building of more Confucian shrines and renovated the Confucian's home

Above: The Praying Hall in Beijing, renamed as the Temple of Heaven by Aisin-Gioro Yongyan.

Left: A firearm, made in England, and used as a gift for Aisin-Gioro Yongyan. *(The Palace Museum)*

town. His policies also revealed his conservatism and righteousness.

One of the first actions he took was to arrest Hongli's favorite chancellor, Heshen. He publicized Heshen's offences of corruption, executed him, and repossessed his wealth, which was said to be the sum of many years of the tax income of the Qing Dynasty.

Left: One of Yongyan's first tasks on becoming emperor was to root out corruption, and in particular he arrested and ordered the execution of Heshen, Hongli's favorite chancellor. *(The Palace Museum)*

Emperor Qing Daoguang

(1782–1850)
Name: Aisin-Gioro Minning
Memorial name: Qing Xuanzong

While China reached her peak in the 18th Century, Chinese products were well known by the Europeans. Tea, silk, porcelain, art and craft works all continued to travel afar via the Silk Road and sea routes. As European traders became increasingly hungry for Chinese products, the empty boats returning back to China were problematic and dissatisfying. Opium was first introduced to the Chinese, but it was banned by the emperor. However, the traders were also invaders. They did not stop their aggression.

Minning inherited his throne during this turbulent time. Domestically, China was a melting pot

Right: When Emperor Qing Daoguang ascended the throne the country was in turmoil, with frequent outbursts of violence at the borders, rebellions, and forceful attempts at independence from local ethnic groups. But possibly an even greater threat to China's stability was the insidious introduction of opium by Westerners, and the attempts to stem its flow, in what came to be called the "Opium Wars." (The Palace Museum)

of many ethnic groups, thanks to the Mongolians and Manchurians themselves. Local ethnic groups around the borders voiced their wishes to be independent. Rebellions and regional fighting occurred frequently. There were no signs of it stopping; indeed it accelerated. While Minning was busy putting out the fires, opium, although a banned addictive drug, continued to flow in. Traders took advantage of the loopholes through the corrupt officers to ship greater volumes of it into China's mainland.

The administration was polarized. On the one hand, there were officers who strongly believed this was just a key for the Europeans to enter China until they conquered the nation; on the other hand, the emperor was lobbied by his closest chancellors, who were afraid of confronting the Westerners. Minning was decisive in assigning Chancellor Lin Zexu to be the Special Envoy to investigate the port trading system, blocking ships with opium from docking in Chinese ports.

Lin Zexu succeeded. Millions of pounds of opium were seized through the investigations and publicly destroyed in 1839. It brought a round of applause and raised hope in the society. But this action could have been just what the British "traders" were looking for. In 1840, the British sailed into the China Sea, this time not for trading but to open fire on the Chinese, who were experienced only in foot or horseback fighting. Not only losing on the battle front, but internally as well, the emperor was pressured to give in, avoiding more wars.

After lengthy negotiations, the "Nanjing Treaty" was signed, marking the end of the Opium War. The Chinese lost the battle, money, Hong Kong, and control over the ports of Guangzhou and Shanghai. The emperor thought he bought peace for the court and civilians but this was merely the beginning of a long war that would last for decades.

Minning worked hard, as he had been educated to do. As the Europeans had sped up their development since the Industrial Revolution, his power was far less significant, compared to the steam engines, in turning China's fate around. The loss led the Qing Dynasty one step closer to its end.

Below: A blue glass bowl etched with a butterfly, from the Daoguang era, *(The Palace Museum)*

Emperor Qing Xianfeng

(1831–1861)
Name: Aisin-Gioro Yizhu
Memorial name: Qing Wenzong

After Hongli, the emperor who brought the Qing Dynasty to its peak, all emperors, even those said to be the Sons of Heaven, were born to fail. When the Opium War broke out, Yizhu was only nine years old. After the "Nanjing Treaty," more Europeans were looking for a piece of this ancient country that they had admired for centuries.

In 1858, the European united army, led by the British and French, landed in the port of Tianjin and marched right into Beijing. Yizhu took off to Rehe, Palace Resort. He sent his troops to defend the city, but without guns and canons all fighting was in vain. With the emperor's absence and no effective defense, the Europeans took whatever they could, set fires, and occupied Beijing. Another treaty was signed on the emperor's behalf, more lands were sacrificed, and more treasures were given away. Yizhu in the meantime died of exhaustion from his extravagant life-style, never having returned to Beijing.

Above: Aisin-Gioro Yizhu (Emperor Qing Xianfeng) did not stay to defend Beijing from the foreign (mostly British and French) invaders, but fled the city, never to return. *(The Palace Museum)*

180

Dowager Ci'xi
(1835–1908)
Name: Yehe-Nala Lan'er

A concubine, empress, widow, mother, and dowager, Ci'xi was all of those, and her power could match that of many emperors in history. She was born into a Manchurian family that was not well off because of her father's early death. She was chosen and brought into the palace as a concubine of Yizhu at the fifth rank, serving other empresses. She was soon pregnant and gave birth to a son, who was named Aisin-Gioro Zaitian. With the first son of Yizhu, she was promoted to an empress and given the name Ci'xi.

Beijing was under attack by the Europeans. Ci'xi accompanied her husband and son, escaping to Rehe. The emperor would never return; he died in Rehe. The death of her husband brought Ci'xi both sorrow and fear. She feared that she would lose her priority position and the power that came with the fact that she was the mother of the heir-apparent. Eight chancellors appointed by the previous emperor represented a group of some strength. She would soon be alienated from the emperor or eliminated. Before her husband Yizhu died, she was given a key as a seal of authority to be used in an emergency for her son and herself. With this key she quickly made allies of Empress Ci'an, whose rank was above her, and her brother-in-law Aisin-Gioro Yixin. Within two months, they cracked the alliance of the eight chancellors, overthrowing their authority in a coup in 1861.

With her son inaugurated as an emperor at only six years of age, Ci'xi volunteered to administer the country. Thousands of years of history and culture had written, however, that no women were allowed in the political arena. This did not stop Ci'xi. A curtain behind her son's

Above: Ci'xi, a tough and wily politician, the real power behind the throne for decades in the 19th Century. *(The Palace Museum)*

throne isolated her from being present in the administration court. But she could listen, talk, sign, and rule.

The situation became the more dramatic when she found out that her previous emperor husband had also offered a seal to Dowager Ci'an; Ci'xi's authority would be validated only if paired with Ci'an's seal. In partnership, Ci'an and Ci'xi started the period called "Ruling Behind The Curtain."

In 1881, Ci'an suddenly fell ill and died within a day. At

Above: The Summer Palace, Beijing. In the 1880s Dowager Ci'xi diverted funds for its expansion from the budget intended for modernization of the Chinese navy.

the age of four Zaitian was brought into the palace to continue the reign. Being brought up by Dowager Ci'xi, Zaitian was the second emperor who ruled with dowagers behind him. Once he grew up, conflicts developed between him and the dowager. Zaitian attempted a reform

brought to the palace as the selected heir, and he was to become known as the last emperor of China.

At the first Opium War Ci'xi was only five years old. Throughout her life in the palace she had experienced Chinese military failures one after another. Through her, many more unfair treaties were signed, sacrificing China in order to sustain her own centered power and imperial life. Probably the most criticized was her decision to use funds earmarked to establish a modern Chinese navy to instead rebuild the Summer Palace for her retirement. Ci'xi always tried to show herself as open to new ideas. However, when she heard that an

emperor's reform would require her to give up her authority, she managed to halt the reform to ensure her position in the court. Between 1861 and 1908, she was the real ruler of China.

An American painter, Katharine Carl, who created the portrait for the dowager, once described her as "...a kind and considerate woman for her station. Dowager Ci'xi, though shrewd, had great presence, charm, and graceful movements resulting in an unusually attractive personality. She loved dogs and had a kennel maintained by eunuchs at the Summer Palace...".

Above: One of Dowager Ci'xi's perfume dispensers. (The Palace Museum)

Right: Stone Boathouse, Dowager Ci'xi's favorite, was built in 1755. After it was destroyed by the European invaders, Ci'xi ordered it to be rebuilt in the Western style.

to restructure the bureaucracy that included his mother. It failed when his military backup flipped to the dowager's conservative side at the last moment. He was then imprisoned and was never forgiven until his death. At Dowager Ci'xi's deathbed (at age seventy-two), Puyi was

Emperor Qing Tongzhi

(1856–1874)
Name: Aisin-Gioro Zaichun
Memorial name: Ming Muzong

After Yizhu died when Beijing was under attack, his six-year-old son took over the tough responsibility of the emperor. There were mountainous problems waiting for him. Yizhu had assigned his eight most trusted chancellors to support the young emperor who would be carrying on the problematic reign, which was in great danger. The internal battle seemed to be more vicious than wars against the Europeans. Within months, all eight chancellors were fired and executed on the orders of Dowagers Ci'an and Ci'xi..

Dowager Ci'an, head of the empresses, was Yizhu's first wife, while Ci'xi was the mother of Zaichun, the only surviving son of the emperor and her. Ci'xi was well recognized as an educated and influential figure at the time. The two widows, allied with Prince Gong, Yixi, the brother of their husband, took over the administration through the "Yinyou Coup" (Yinyou was the calendar name of the year). The dowagers were not allowed in the political arena. They sat behind the emperor with a curtain in front of them and supervised the administration from there. The period of "Ruling Behind A Curtain" began.

Zaichun spent most of his reigning period reading and preparing himself for the great responsibilities when he could independently manage the administration. That day arrived in 1873. However, he died of smallpox within a year, although a rumor was that the palace concealed the information that the emperor died of a sexually transmitted disease.

Above: Emperor Qing Tongzhi (Aisin-Gioro Zaichun) grew up under the protective wing of his mother, the powerful Dowager Ci'xi, but died within a year of ascending the throne. *(The Palace Museum)*

Emperor Qing Guangxu

(1871–1908)
Name: Aisin-Gioro Zaitian
Memorial name: Qing Dezong

Zaitian, Dowager Ci'xi's nephew, was quickly brought to the throne after Zaichun's death. Having died at a young age, Zaichun did not leave any heir. The dowager chose Zaitian, the son of her husband's nephew and her own sister, to inherit the Qing Dynasty. He was only four years old. Obviously, the young emperor would need further manipulation from the experienced dowagers.

In the meantime, China fell deeper and deeper into turmoil. Along with natural disasters including floods, locusts, and droughts and the already threatening European invasion, came the Japanese. In 1894 Japan invaded Korea, which was under the protection of the Qing reign. The administration was distinctively divided into "War and Peace." Zaitian led his side and declared war on the Japanese. The consequence was another military disaster. The Qing navy was sunk during the Japanese attack. Ci'xi led her side and immediately insisted on negotiation. The Qing administration was already familiar with this way of handling the foreign invaders. This time, the Japanese received their piece of China.

The young emperor felt humiliated after the defeat and the unfair treaties enforced by the Japanese and Europeans. His closest chancellors advocated reform, oriented around education, government recruiting, economy, and the restructuring of the government itself. The restructure of course included a gesture of the retirement of Dowager Ci'xi. The news shook the courtiers who had worked around Dowager Ci'xi and who were favored by her. The resistance from inside the palace forced the emperor to prepare for military action. Yuan Shikai, a young and uprising general was selected for such a task. However, at the last second, he surprised everybody by flipping to the dowager's conservative side.

A promising reform, probably the final remedy for the decayed Qing Dynasty, became the motive power for another deadly coup in 1894. The entire process lasted for one hundred days. Historians also call it "A Hundred Day Reform." All reformers were executed. Dowager Ci'xi could not forgive Zaitian's slightest thought of ever using force on her. She isolated and imprisoned him in Yingtai Palace. It was here that Zaitian died with regret, disappointment, and hatred.

Left: Emperor Qing Guangxu (Aisin-Gioro Zaitian), who faced up to the Japanese invaders, but was imprisoned by a dowager, Ci'xi. *(The Palace Museum)*

Far left: An elaborately embroidered. gold-buttoned vest/waistcoat made for the young Emperor Qing Guangxu. *(The Palace Museum)*

Emperor Qing Xuantong

(1906–1967)
Name: Aisin-Gioro Puyi
Memorial name: Gongzong (unapproved)

Puyi became known throughout the world as the Last Emperor. In 1987, Italian movie director Bernardo Bertolucci launched a global blockbuster named "The Last Emperor" to review Puyi's life as a child, emperor, and an ordinary citizen in China. His life was indeed very dramatic.

Zaitian, imprisoned and dead at a young age, did not leave the court with an heir. In 1908, Puyi, another member of the Aisin-Gioro bloodline, was brought into the palace to attend Dowager Ci'xi's deathbed. His inauguration took place at the age of three without him understanding why his new home was the Forbidden City. Brought up by his father, then his chancellor, Puyi was educated to believe that he was the son of heaven and had been given power to rule China.

The political situation in China was way more complicated than he was told. In 1911, outside the Forbidden City, liberal revolutionist Sun Yat-sen (also Sun Yixian) established the Republic of China and became its first provisional president. Dowager Longyu, on behalf of the Qing Dynasty and the emperor, handed him the "Act of Abdication of the Emperor of the Great Qing." Thus ended the Qing's sovereignty. As part of the concession agreement, the imperial family stayed in the palace. Puyi continued his emperor's life-style in the meantime. In 1924, reality was brought home when warlord Feng Yuxiang drove the palace resident out, forcing Puyi to be exiled. The Qing was diminished.

The young Puyi, whom the remnants of the Qing expected would become emperor, sought asylum. Sun Yat-sen died in 1925 and China was in a state of disarray, being carved up by warlords, the Republic, and Japanese and Western invaders. Under Japanese "protection," Puyi returned to his ancestors' home town in the northeast. His dream of becoming emperor was fulfilled with the help of the Japanese when they established the State of Manchuria. This was, in a real sense, a colony of Japan and Puyi was merely a puppet the Japanese used as a screen to hide their plan to conquer the rest of China. This intention was made evident shortly after, when they started to invade other provinces in China. In 1937, they marched into Beijing, marking the beginning of their official invasion. Puyi was kept as a hostage until the end of the anti-Japanese war in 1945, when he was seized as a war prisoner by the Soviet Union.

Puyi dreaded the Chinese communists, but Russia's leader, Stalin, rejected his requests to stay in the Soviet Union. Puyi was returned and kept in the Fushun War Criminal Management Center in China until 1950. He was released in 1959 and was offered citizenship by the People's Republic of China. In 1962, he remarried under the law of the Republic. He also developed a career, devoting his last years to helping Chinese historians research the Qing Dynasty. Before he died, he managed to publish his own autobiography, *The First Half of My Life,"* also known in English as *"From Emperor to Citizen."* In 1969, the last emperor and ordinary Chinese citizen died of kidney cancer.

Left: Aisin-Gioro Puyi, the "Last Emperor," at the inauguration of the Manchu State after the collapse of the Qing Dynasty in 1911. *(The Palace Museum)*

Right: Aisin-Gioro Puyi's opulent sitting room in the Forbidden City.

Index